Great Parties for Young Children

Great Parties for Young Children

CHERYL CARTER BARRON
and
CATHY CARMICHAEL SCHERZER

Illustrated by Cathy Carmichael Scherzer

Walker and Company 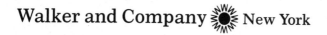 New York

First published in the United States of America in 1981 by the Walker Publishing Company, Inc.

Published simultaneously in Canada by John Wiley & Sons Canada, Limited, Rexdale, Ontario.

ISBN: 0-807-0684-3 (cloth)
          0-807-7175-0 (paper)

Library of Congress Catalog Card Number: 81-50232

Printed in the United States of America

10 9 8 7 6 5 4 3 2 1

BOOK DESIGN: RFS GRAPHIC DESIGN, INC.

*To our children, Sam, Kacey, Betsy and
Chris, who inspired us. To our husbands, Steve
and Jerry, who supported us. To our mothers, Sue
and Rose, and our fathers, Mike and Rollie, who
gave us wonderful parties and much, much more.*

A children's party can be cleaned up in a few minutes, but a beautiful memory lasts a lifetime.

Contents

Introduction

Stop for a minute and think of the one party that stands out in your childhood memories. Remember the wonderful feeling you had that day and the wonderful feeling you have right now just thinking about it. Don't you want to give that feeling to your child? A party should reflect happiness and, most of all, love.

We each have a child with a December 29th birthday. One day we were discussing how sad it was that our children's birthdays are in the shadow of Christmas and that we would really have to make their birthday parties very special. It was then that we realized that *any* and *every* children's party should be as special as can be!

Although the most frequent children's party is a birthday party, there are many other reasons for having one. You may want to celebrate a holiday—Valentine's Day, St. Patrick's Day, Easter, Fourth of July, Christmas, Hallowe'en or Thanksgiving, or just the end of the school year. Welcoming a new neighbor or introducing a friend are also reasons for having a party. And then there are no-reason-at-all parties.

Through our research, we found that there was very little written about parties for very young children. Yet parents of younger children are the most in need of suggestions and guidance for this new adventure.

With this in mind, we set out to catalog ideas and suggestions that will serve moms and dads as well as act as a catalyst for creating parties their children will remember fondly.

We hope this book will help you create your child's most "unforgettable" party.

The Authors

Every party is unique. It takes on the flavor and color of the host or hostess. There are certain characteristics that make the party yours. To ensure your party is as much fun and as entertaining as you have planned, we offer a few suggestions. The following is a list of ideas for your consideration so you won't have to learn by your mistakes. We call them:

1

Things You Thought You Knew, but You'll Be Glad You Read About Anyway

TIME LIMIT

Unless you are taking older children to a skating rink, movie theater, etc., a party should not last more than two hours. It is wise to state the length of the party on the invitation so parents will know when to return for pickup. A little trick if you want to make sure the party ends on time is to tell the parents you will bring each child home.

LIMIT THE NUMBER OF GUESTS

If you live in a child-oriented neighborhood or have lots of relatives who live close by, limiting your guests will be a problem. We suggest setting a rule of one guest for every year plus one (five guests on the fourth birthday, six on the fifth, etc.). If you really feel you will be breaking some hearts, make a deal with a friend whereby she takes the leftover children and siblings to the park for a picnic. Then you can pay her back on her child's special day. Occasionally, a daddy will volunteer for this duty.

SIBLINGS

If you are giving a birthday party, that should be the one day when your child does not have to compete with anybody. Brothers and sisters may be invited to the party if you feel they will not cause a problem. However, if there is any possibility that they will try to steal the show, make other arrangements. Have your other children go to a neighbor's house for the day or to the movies with Daddy, etc. As for your guests' siblings, make it clear who is invited to the party and hope that your friends will not bring an uninvited guest. An exception, of course, would be an infant who is still breast-feeding but promises to be unobtrusive!

EARLY ARRIVALS/LATE DEPARTURES

A wise hostess will plan on the unexpected. Guests, unfortunately, do not usually arrive en masse. It is a good idea to have an activity planned for each child as he arrives. Each party in subsequent chapters will give you ideas on arrival activities. It is also smart to have some coloring books, etc., on hand for that last child whose mother is still at the shopping center and has lost track of time.

PARTY HELPERS

Don't be a martyr. Enlist the aid of your spouse, neighbor, mother, etc. Parties are "high" times, and a great deal of supervision is necessary to insure success. The first and second birthdays will include the guests' mothers, but after that you will probably be on your own. As the children get older, you won't want a lot of adults standing around anyway; but a little help is vital. You may wish to hire your child's favorite sitter to help with games as well as cleanup. Discuss your plans ahead of time with your helper so she'll know just what is expected of her. Remember that teenage boys love children as much as teenage girls and make excellent helpers.

BACKGROUND MUSIC

Music sets the mood for any party. It is fun to have lively music for running games and other outdoor activities. It is nice to have quiet music for quiet activities. Soft classical music during lunch helps to maintain a soothing atmosphere. There are also many activity and sing-along records available at your public library or record store.

STORIES

Sometimes parties can get a little out of hand or have an undesired lull. In each of these cases, a short story read with lots of expression can save the day (or the party). It's a unifying factor that has a calming yet stimulating effect.

A highly successful way to attract the children's attention is to whisper. You may wish to use this tactic simply to calm the party down or to explain a game. (Children respond and listen to whispering better than screaming.)

Try to tie the story in with the theme if you can. Remember that children of all ages like to be read to. Your librarian can be a great resource person for expressive short stories.

BALLOONS

Balloons add a festive touch to every birthday party. Always plan on plenty of breakage. Allow for two or three balloons per guest if you want one to serve as a favor upon departure. Helium balloons are especially fun. Check the Yellow Pages of your phone book under "Gases, Industrial" for the location of an outlet in your area. Helium balloons should be kept indoors or tied securely around the child's wrist or ankle. A bunch of helium balloons tied together, secured to a picnic table, makes a good outdoor centerpiece. Broken bits of balloons should be kept away from babies.

PRIZES

A party's goal is for everyone to have fun. Competition is healthy, but it need not be rewarded. We choose not to give prizes with our games. The younger children don't expect them, and the older children can be told that the games are being played for fun.

If you choose to give prizes, make sure that everyone receives one. (You may have to search for reasons, though!) Our suggested party favors can serve as prizes.

FAVORS

As we will mention later, a specially wrapped favor for each guest is important. If you have the time, a homemade gift is best, made by your child or by the guest during the party. Be sure the favors are all alike in size, visual appeal, etc. to avoid conflict. Also allow time and space for the guests to enjoy their favors.

CANDLES

For a birthday, candles are a must. However, they can be dangerous. Watch out for children with long hair or loose-fitting clothing. Children under the age of three often do not understand the presence of danger. You may have to practice blowing out candles and candle safety prior to the party.

PHOTOGRAPHS

There are many ways to preserve a special day. Photographs are certainly at the top of the list. Be sure to take lots of snapshots before, during and even after the party. A camera with a self-developer can be fun as the guests can also enjoy them. Home movies are super and make for years of entertainment. The movie camera, as well as projector and screen, can be rented from a camera shop at a reasonable cost. Another idea is to tape-record parts or all of the party (with or without the guests' knowledge).

Some baby books have pages to fill in party details,

or you may wish to set aside one photo album just to record your child's parties over the years. It would be enjoyable to look back and see what your parties were like, guests, decorations, gifts received and menus.

GIFTS

Gift giving is an old and treasured custom of our culture. It is a beautiful way to express good wishes to others. Be sure, however, that your child is sufficiently mature to give and receive gifts. If the gift opening is going to be riddled with jealousy and tears, you may wish to try something different. The first obvious solution is to request "no gifts." This is not very fair to your child, but it is an option. Another solution is to have your child personally wrap a favor for each guest. Then, as the birthday child opens a gift from a friend, he or she will in turn give a gift to that friend and they can open them simultaneously. A third alternative is simply to reserve the gifts for the tail end of the party or after the guests have departed.

THANK YOU

Thank-you notes are very important, especially if you opt to open gifts after the party. If your child is capable, he should write the notes himself. Otherwise, mailing a candid photograph taken of each guest during the party, with "Thank you" written on the back, makes a nice thank you. If during your party you had the children create something special, it is nice to have your child hand-deliver it the next day and say thank you in person.

Birthday Parties for Toddlers— One- and Two-Year-Olds

Birthdays are special! The first birthday may be more special for you as a parent. After all, it is the anniversary of one of the most memorable days in your life. Celebrating the first birthday is a family affair. You may wish to have a quiet dinner with cake, ice cream and lots of pictures. Or you may wish to include a few relatives and friends to drink a toast to the guest of honor.

Psychologists tell us that a person's memory goes back to the onset of expressive language. So the extent to which your child is talking can be directly proportionate to how "unforgettable" his party will be. But remember, special memories are created and easily preserved through photographs and reminiscences.

7

A party doesn't need to be elaborate. It can be quite simple and inexpensive. We offer many do-it-yourself ideas to make your party unique.

So have a party for your child every year . . . starting with Year One.

There are three things to keep in mind for a toddler's party: limit the guests, limit the time and plan for moms. Hopefully, none of your friends will drop her toddler on your doorstep and head for the nearest tennis court or home for some peace and quiet. In order to prevent this, invite the moms for lunch or a glass of wine. The lunch hour is a good time for a party because working moms and dads can come and the children will be ready for naps after lunch, so your guests will be sure to leave before things get out of hand!

A late afternoon party is also a good idea because the children are fresh from their naps, but they won't stay too late due to the approaching dinner hour. And, too, parents can stop by on their way home from work. (Daddies like birthday parties, too!)

A third option may be to have your party on a weekend, but you might miss some special friends who have previous weekend plans.

Be sure to invite only as many guests as your house and sanity can accommodate. If there are siblings involved, it is better to be prepared than surprised when they show up.

One- and two-year-olds respond to bright colors and movement. Make the party a visual one. Carry out a bright but simple color scheme. One color is best.

The invitations should be telephoned because you have a lot to tell the mothers. Besides making sure that each mother plans on attending the party, let her know that you'll be expecting her assistance with her own child. Ask her to bring her child's high chair if possible. Set the chairs in a circle like the "Knights of the Round High Chairs." If the high chairs present a problem, a

8

coffee table makes a great eating surface. Have each guest bring his own little chair or borrow them ahead of time from friends.

A piece of fabric makes an attractive tablecloth. (Fabric remnants are less expensive than paper cloths and infinitely better.) A simple centerpiece is a delightful touch; try a bunch of wild flowers or something from your garden or vegetable bin (parsley, broccoli, carrot tops, etc.) in your child's silver cup. Brightly colored salad-size paper plates are effective, or you may wish to use inexpensive white ones and decorate them with nontoxic felt-tipped pens. These plates can also double as place cards.

Streamers and helium balloons with extra long strings reaching to the floor make indoor decorations simple yet colorful. Get enough balloons to allow for lots of "poppage." A helium balloon's life expectancy is approximately four hours. Take this into consideration when planning your party! The extra long strings make it easy for a walking or crawling one-year-old to grab them without help from Mom. (Balloons can also be tied to feet or shoes!) You'll be surprised at what a hit these balloons will be.

Party hats and favors are a must. Birthday hats are easy to make from paper. Use your imagination or try our idea in the chapter called "Clowns, Clowns, Clowns." But don't get hurt feelings if not all the guests share your enthusiasm for these hats.

A charming favor idea is a personalized bib for each guest. Buy a package of inexpensive cloth bibs and iron on an initial or name either out of scraps in your sewing bag or precut iron-ons. Or, on doubled fabric, simply trace around one of your child's bibs and cut out two pieces per bib. Place the right sides together and pin. Insert two pieces of ribbon or bias tape at the neck and stitch. Turn the bib right side out and write the child's name on it with crayon. Cover the writing with a piece of

9

brown paper bag and iron. This will lift the wax and leave the color permanently. These bibs are invaluable at the party and a special favor for your guests.

The menu for your party should be simple and nutritious. We suggest the following menu for the children. (You'll find recipes in the last chapter.)

Chain-O-Lunch
Grilled Cheese Loverlies
Juice
Yogurt Balls
Carrot Cupcakes

Most toddlers are not big eaters, so keep your menu simple. The kids with heartier appetites will help clean off the table after the picky eaters have retired to play. Whether you choose to serve lunch or simply cake and ice cream, it should be nutritious and appealing. Your color scheme can be carried through the menu to add to the festive atmosphere (as well as the "oohs and aahs" of your friends).

The mothers will be hungry, too. So set up a nice sandwich or salad bar away from the hubbub, where they can eat at their convenience.

The lunch will be the highlight of the party, so relax and enjoy it. After lunch the children will want to play. You may wish to have the birthday child open gifts at this time, unless you feel it would cause problems.

Don't try to plan any structured activities for toddlers. Simply let them eat and play. You might ask each mom to bring one of her child's favorite toys to share at the party. An unfamiliar toy can insure a longer-than-normal playtime for a curious toddler. You may want to remove some furniture in order to increase the size of the play area. Remember to remove any treasure you wouldn't want broken!

Limiting the length of your party will probably not

be a problem at this point, as no one will be able to stand the chaos when the party has gone on too long.

Speaking of chaos, this will be a fun-filled day, but a draining one. Have a sitter lined up for the evening so you can go out for a nice dinner after the children are tucked into bed. Remember, this is your special day, too!

If you do have gifts brought to the party, a nice thank-you-note idea is a footprint or handprint of the birthday child on the front of a piece of note paper. Either trace the hand or foot and cut out the form as a pattern or rub the child's hand or foot in water-based poster paints and stamp on paper. Add your thank-you message and mail. The result is a darling personal note.

Three-Year-Olds

Traditional Birthday Party

This is a good time to have a really traditional birthday party, because your child is old enough to remember the party but not the details. Therefore, simplicity and "Sunday Best" are the keys.

Here is our rendition of the classic birthday party, complete with polished shoes and hair ribbons!

INVITATIONS

Let your child choose the invitations from a stationery store, variety store, etc.

DECORATIONS

Helium balloons and crepe paper streamers can really set the mood. If you want to have the party outdoors, secure the balloons to the back of each chair and write the children's names on them (see "Clowns, Clowns, Clowns" invitations).

CENTERPIECE: A traditional round layer cake lusciously frosted with colored whipped cream and decorated with fresh daisies and sprigs of parsley makes a delicious centerpiece.

TABLECLOTH: Use a complementing and colorful flat sheet.

PLACECARD: Tie a bright ribbon and name tag through a doughnut.

MENU

Tuna Burgers or Tuna Boats
Finger Veggies (olives, carrots, pickles)
Banana slices rolled in granola (see
    Bananaships)
Yogurt Shake

13

Basket of cookies
Glass bowl filled with ice cream, yogurt or
   sherbet scoops

CAKE

Traditional round layer cake. If you really want to make it special, wait for the layers to cool and slice each layer in half, giving you four layers. Fill with frosting, whipped cream, instant pudding or jam. To these you can add candy, marshmallows, nuts, etc. It's fun to have each layer different and a surprise. Frost the outside generously and make sure that your child's name is boldly visible.

COSTUMES

"Sunday Best"—have children wear their "Special Occasion Outfit."

ACTIVITIES

Mom or helpers put on a puppet show (see "Puppets" for ideas).

GAMES

Pin-the-Tail-on-the-Donkey
Penny Hunt
Go Fish
Drop the Clothespin
(See "Games" for additional ideas)

FAVORS

Go for the tried-and-true traditional: whistles, noisemakers, balloons, party hats, candy cups and small, inexpensive cardboard-covered books.

TAKE HOMES

Fold an 8½″ × 11″ piece of colored paper or gift wrap in half. Turn up two open sides ½″ and staple. This makes a nice bag with a colorful touch.

THANK YOU

If you think your three-year-old is capable, have him or her phone the guests the next day and thank them for coming to the party. This is a marvelous opportunity to work on telephone manners.

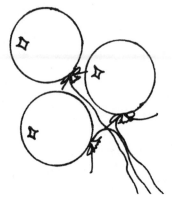

Boy/Girl 4, 5, 6

Clowns, Clowns, Clowns

This party is great for getting the children actively involved and interacting with each other. After all, we all have a bit of the clown in us, don't we?

INVITATIONS

1) Blow up a balloon, but do not tie it. Using a ballpoint pen*, write the invitation information on the balloon. Let it dry for a minute, then release the air. Place the balloon in an envelope and distribute.

2) Bouncing Clown. Fold a piece of white paper in half. On the upper half, print the party information. On the

*We experimented with all sorts of felt pens, etc, and found ballpoints work best.

lower half in the center, attach a 4″ accordioned strip of paper. To the end of the strip, attach a clown face (drawn on white paper and cut out). The clown will then bounce out at the invitee when the invitation is opened.

DECORATIONS

The color scheme is most effective if you use bright, rainbow colors.

CENTERPIECE: Group five helium balloons together and tie the strings to a rock. Stuff an old white glove with cotton to resemble a hand. Wrap the "hand" around the base of the tied balloons. The effect should be a clown's hand holding balloons.

  Note: Helium balloons can be found by looking in the Yellow Pages of your phone book under "Gases, Industrial." Keep in mind that a helium balloon's life expectancy is approximately four hours.

PLACECARD: Puzzle Cookie (see additional arrival activities)

PLACE MAT/TABLECLOTH: Use a white sheet for a tablecloth. Place 11″ round cut-out circles from multicolored construction paper (11″ × 15″) as placemats.

GENERAL DECORATIONS:

    1) Suspend a large sheet from the center of the ceiling with a small nail and attach the corners to the walls to give a "Big Top" effect.
    2) Suspend clown face drawings from the ceiling or hang on walls.
    3) Let helium balloons of various colors hang from the ceiling.

17

MENU

Grease Paint Sandwiches
Apple Rings
Carrot and celery sticks
Clown Cones
Mmmmm Goods

CAKE

Clown Cake

ARRIVAL ACTIVITY

Using our Grease Paint recipe (page 125), inexpensive dark lipstick and liquid eyeliner, paint each child with a clown face. Great ideas can be found in clown books at the library. Take your child along to pick out his or her favorite clowns.

ADDITIONAL ACTIVITIES

When one child is being painted, have the other children work on the *Cookie Puzzle*:

Prepare a sugar cookie recipe. As soon as cookies come out of the oven, score with a knife where you want the divisions to be (but don't cut all the way through). Let the cookies cool thoroughly. When cooled, break at divisions and place a letter on each piece with tube frosting.

Lay out the cookie pieces on a tray. Mix the pieces up and have each child find his/her name and take it to his/her place at the table.

CLOWN'S COLLAR: Buy a package of brightly colored sheet crepe paper. Leave it folded and cut into 6" strips. Using a needle, push a 20" piece of thread through the paper. Knot at each end, tie the collar around the child's neck and work it around like a ruffle.

CLOWN HAT: Cut a piece of paper 24" in diameter. Cut a line from the edge to the center. Draw the ends around until you arrive at a cone shape. Staple. Punch two holes at the bottom of the cone on opposite sides. Attach yarn "straps" to each hole.

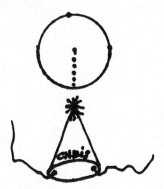

Make a yarn pompon by wrapping yarn ten to fifteen times around your four fingers. Tie at the center. Snip ends and "fluff." Staple the tassle to the tip of the hat. Write each child's name on the hats with felt pen or crayon.

GAMES

Bean Bag Toss
Shoe Race
Pin-the-Nose-on-the-Clown

19

FAVORS

1) Self-developing photograph of each child as a clown (rent or borrow the camera)
2) Balloons of all shapes and sizes
3) Plastic or rubber balls

TAKE HOMES

Staple the self-developing photo to one side of a paper lunch bag. Each child will then have a personalized bag in which to carry home his favors, prizes and treats.

THANK YOU

Write "Thank you for coming to my party" on the back of each take home bag.

Boy/Girl 4, 5, 6

The rich cultural heritage that surrounds Native Americans would make this an excellent Thanksgiving party.

INVITATIONS

Write your invitation on the outside of a small brown paper bag. (You may want to fringe the top.) White chalk and black felt tip marker look best, but colored crayon works just as well. Then simply fold and staple. Ask the children to bring the bag to the party and it will double as a take-home bag.

DECORATIONS

Using colored, nontoxic, felt-tip pens, draw an Indian face on a paper plate—one for each guest. Tape a bright paper headband across the top and stick in a feather.

Hang the plates on the wall with straight steel pins* and let each child choose his favorite when it's time to eat. (You may have to remind them this is a "Peace Party"!)

CENTERPIECE: Fill a basket with popcorn balls on sticks (see "Recipes") and stick a few feathers here and there for color.

PLACECARD: Make a miniature tee-pee by turning a sugar cone upside down. Use a frosting decorating tube (located near the cake mixes in the grocery store) to write each child's name down the middle.

PLACE MAT: Cut place-mat size rectangles from large brown grocery bags. Fringe the edges and decorate with Indian symbols.

MENU

Paper canoe* filled with nuts, seeds, raisins, etc.
Corn on the cob (fresh or frozen)
Chili-corn Cups
Apple slices
Apple juice

CAKE

Totem Pole Cake

---

*Steel pins, not silk pins, can be lightly hammered into most walls and will not leave a mark. (We use them to hang pictures, etc.—they're great!)

*Paper canoe: Fold but *do not crease* a 5½" × 8½" piece of brown construction paper (one half sheet) lengthwise. Staple the ends.

ARRIVAL ACTIVITY

Cut a large neck opening in the bottom of a big grocery bag. Then cut holes on either side for the arms and a slit up the back. Fringe the bottom. As each guest arrives, give him or her a costume to color and decorate with scraps of paper, glue, beads, feathers, macaroni, color crayons, etc. Complete the outfit with a paper headband and feather (call a poultry wholesaler if you have trouble finding feathers). The boys may prefer a loin cloth, which is also easy to make. Just cut two pieces from a brown paper bag, fringe, fold each over a long piece of yarn, staple and decorate. Place one "cloth" in front and one in back and tie yarn together at the sides.

After all the guests have arrived and are busily working on their costumes, go around and make each child up with "Peace Paint" (see Grease Paint in "Activities").

ADDITIONAL ACTIVITIES

Make a tom-tom using a cardboard ice cream tub from an ice cream parlor. Decorate the outside, turn it upside down and beat!

String colored macaroni to make beautiful Indian beads. Color uncooked salad macaroni by putting it in a jar, adding a few drops of food coloring and a splash of vinegar. Shake. Spread on waxed paper to dry. Make several colors. String on thread or yarn.

If you live near a wooded area, take the children on a nature walk to gather leaves, acorns, pine cones, etc. Ask the children what they think Indian life was like.

Peace Pipe Bubbles—see "Activities."

GAMES

Cheyenne Charades
Rain Dance

FAVORS

Make a tomahawk shaker for each child with a discarded toilet paper roll. Cover the ends with a small circle of cloth and secure with rubber bands. Fill with a tablespoon of dried beans. Stick a tongue depressor (available at a drugstore) in the side for a handle. Run a little white glue around the entry point so that the shaker won't fall off the stick.

TAKE HOMES

See Invitations

THANK YOU

See Favors

START SAVING THOSE GROCERY BAGS!!!

6

Girls 4, 5, 6

Hearts Galore

This is an adorable party for your adorable little girl . . . with a red-and-white color scheme and hearts galore! It is a natural for a Valentine's Day party.

INVITATIONS

Cut a string of hearts "Paper-doll style"* out of red paper. Write each piece of information on a different heart.

*Accordion pleat the paper. Cut a heart shape, leaving a small section on each side connected.

DECORATIONS

Festoon the ceiling with white helium balloons and red crepe paper streamers. Let the balloon strings dangle and tie a red or pink paper heart on the end of each one.

CENTERPIECE: Hearts 'n Flowers—put a small plastic margarine tub in the bottom of a basket. Fill the bowl with a few wound-up flower stems or oasis and water. Intersperse red paper hearts glued on pipe cleaners and white daisies.

PLACECARD:

> *ANN'S SPECIAL PLACECARD COOKIES*
> Using either store-bought refrigerator cookies or our sugar cookie recipe, roll out dough and cut with heart-shaped cookie cutter. Punch two "hole-puncher" size holes at the top with a toothpick. Follow recipe baking instructions. Cool. Decorate with each guest's name spelled in icing from a decorating tube. String yarn through the holes so the cookie can double as a necklace.

Another attractive touch is to put a drinking straw at each place with a personalized heart on it.

PLACE MAT: Cut red hearts from a large piece of construction paper (11″ × 15″). You may wish to use place mats alone, in which case a little doily "lace" glued around the heart is nice, or place the hearts around a white tablecloth.

MENU

Raggamuffins
Sliced Bananas or Strawberries (in season)
Raggedy Ann Cones
Razzamatazz

CAKE

Heart Cake

ARRIVAL ACTIVITY

BALLOON FACES: Supply guests with blown-up balloons, glue, yarn segments (3″ long), ribbon and ball point pens. Have each guest draw her version of Raggedy Ann with ball point pen. She can then glue on the yarn hair and a hair ribbon. As each girl is working, paint a Raggedy Ann face on her with homemade grease paint (see "Activities").

GAMES

Musical Hearts
Copy Cat Dance
Watch Where You Sit!
Drop the Doily (see Duck Duck Goose)
I Love You Line-up (see Spelling Scramble)

27

ADDITIONAL ACTIVITIES

DANGLING COOKIES: In lieu of the cookie necklaces, hang the cookies on a long string attached to the ceiling with a thumbtack. Make sure the strings are long enough for children to reach the cookies with their mouths. With their hands behind their backs, have the children try to eat the cookies. They may need to team up!

VALENTINE BASKETS: Cut red or pink 8½″ × 11″ construction paper down the middle to make two 4¼″ × 11″ pieces for each guest. Fold each piece in half and round off ends (see Diagram). Separate the two pieces and put them back together at an angle to form a heart shape. Have the guests glue or staple them to make a basket. Add a paper handle.

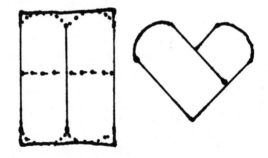

FAVORS

Miniature Raggedy Ann Dolls and other Raggedy Ann paraphernalia, available at the dime store, and Raggedy Ann books.

TAKE HOMES

White paper bag with "I Love You" surrounded by a heart written in red felt marker.

THANK YOU

A box of "Red Hot" cinnamon candies with a thank-you note wrapped around it.

If you are looking for an excuse for a party, why not celebrate your pet's birthday?

Boy/Girl 4, 5, 6

Pet Parade

All children love animals, alive or stuffed. If you're really brave (or out of your tree), ask each guest to bring a pet . . . no horses, please! Or you can simply suggest they bring a favorite stuffed animal to show off. Ask them to dress their pets up (ribbons, etc.) or to dress in a special costume to match their pet.

INVITATIONS

One of our ideas requires a bit of artistic talent, the other does not. Our puppy dog invitation entails drawing a dog's face on construction paper. Cut it out. Cut a tongue from a separate piece of paper. Make a slit in the face and slide the tongue through from the back. Write the party particulars on the ears and tongue.

    The other idea is to write the invitation information on a cloth ribbon (24″ long) with a felt-tip pen. This doubles as a pet collar!

DECORATIONS

There are so many ways to carry out an animal theme, using magazine pictures, dime store cutouts, etc. Buy a package of long skinny balloons and follow the manufacturer's directions on how to make various animals. Tie a piece of yarn to each one and hang from the ceiling with tape.

CENTERPIECE: Fill a basket with yarn pompons and pet toys as well as boxes of animal cookies (see Favors).

PLACECARD-TABLECLOTH: Have the children decorate an old sheet with portraits of their pets (see Arrival Activity).

MENU

Trail Mix in ice cream cones
Animal Cookies
Animal Salad
Orange-up
Fruit-tail Pops

CAKE

Carousel Cake

ARRIVAL ACTIVITY

Cover your table with an old white sheet. Write each guest's name on the cloth at his or her place in crayon. Give the children each a small box of color crayons and show them to their places at the table. Ask them to draw pictures of their pets on the sheet. After the pictures are completed, cover each with a piece of brown paper bag and iron it a few seconds until the wax melts and lifts. (Be sure to put the warm iron out of reach!) This will make a colorful and permanent reminder of your party.

ADDITIONAL ACTIVITIES

1) *MAKE-a-MONSTER:* Give each child an inverted regular ice cream cone and have them decorate the cones with marshmallow creme (as glue), candies, noodles, raisins, and anything else that would make it look yukky.

2) *PAPER BAG PUPPETS:* see "Activities"

GAMES

Duck, Duck, Goose
Go Fish
Who Am I? (Animals)
Animal Races
Birds Fly (see Simon Says)

FAVORS

Pet toys
Yarn Pompons (see Clown Hats)
Dog biscuits
Catnip, bird seed, etc. tied up in a little piece
   of cloth with a ribbon
Crayons

TAKE HOMES

Make a "doggie bag" for each guest by simply writing on
a lunch-size bag.

THANK YOU

Write "Thank you" on a small recipe card with honey or
white glue. Sprinkle with bird seed. Punch two holes at
the top and tie with a ribbon.

Tell the child to tie it to a tree at home to feed the birds!

Children are fascinated with space exploration. Decorations for this party are easy. All you need is a can of silver spray paint and some aluminum foil.

Boy/Girl 4, 5, 6

INVITATIONS

Cut 7″ rocket shapes out of construction paper and write the party information on the front. Fold in half and seal with a gold gummed seal and mail.

DECORATIONS

Attach blue and white balloons to furniture and walls, or have helium balloons floating at the ceiling. Tape construction-paper stars and moons to walls, suspended from the ceiling, or attach to balloon strings.

COLOR SCHEME: Silver, red, orange and yellow

CENTERPIECE: This is a hanging rocket centerpiece. Simply attach two ice cream tubs together with masking tape. Add a construction paper cone for the nose of the rocket. Spray with silver spray paint. Attach streamers of yellow, red and orange crepe paper to the inside at the bottom to simulate flames. You may want to add your child's name, age, etc. down the side.

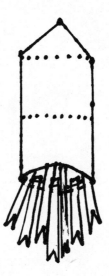

PLACECARD: Make 4″ construction-paper rockets with the children's names on them. Punch two holes in each, one on top and one near the bottom, and slip a straw through the holes. Place in the glass at each place setting.

PLACE MAT: Again the silver theme is dominant. Cover a piece of cardboard (use a laundered shirt cardboard or a gift-box lid) with aluminum foil.

MENU

Moonwich
Bananaships
Moonshine
Yogurt scoops in foil cupcake papers
Blast-offs (commercial yogurt push-ups)

CAKE

Rocket Cake

COSTUMES

Space helmets (see Arrival Activity)

ARRIVAL ACTIVITY

MAKE-YOUR-OWN SPACE HELMET: Using ice cream tubs from your local ice cream parlor, cut out a rectangular space for the eyes and spray the tub silver (this should be done ahead of time).

The decorating supplies for the helmets, along with the glue, can all be placed in the center of the table or in the center of the floor. Remember to use some type of a plastic drop cloth as this could be messy. Empty egg cartons are great supply trays. Fill with sequins, nails, screws, bolts, pipe cleaners, candy kisses, gummed stars, stickers, paper clips, etc. Let the children create their own helmet decorations.

GAMES

Who Am I? (science-fiction heroes)
Space Flight

FAVORS

Helmets, paper airplanes, plastic (store-bought) airplanes

TAKE HOMES

Use helmet as container.

THANK YOU

Distribute star-shaped sugar cookies with "Thank you" written with tube frosting as guests leave for home.

9

This is a super party for children
with a good imagination. It is full
of intrigue and surprise.

Boy/Girl 7, 8, 9   # Whodunnit?

INVITATIONS

Use plain folded note cards. Cover the outside with foot-prints (dip the side of your fist in poster paint, stamp the paper, then add "toes" with your fingertips).

Write the information on the inside in "mirror writing." To do this, hold a piece of paper up to a mirror and write backwards in such a way that you can read it in the mirror.

ꟼLEASE COME

Remember to give them a clue at the bottom of the paper: "Use a mirror!"

DECORATIONS

Cut footprints* out of colored paper and tape them to your floor. Start at the front door and make a path for the children to follow.

CENTERPIECE: Using thread and straight steel pins stuck in the ceiling, dangle "magnifying glasses," "clues" and "question marks" in the center of your table. The magnifying glasses are homemade lollipops (see "Recipes"). The clues are brightly colored cards on which you write: "Under the bed," "Behind the garage," "In the cookie jar," etc. These could be where you have hidden the party favors. Be sure they are wrapped or bagged with the guests' names on them. The question marks are cut out of black construction paper. Run the thread through the top with a needle, then through the dot of the question mark, and tie it.

*Trace your child's foot—cut three or four at once.

40

TABLECLOTH: A few days before your party, spread an old white sheet out on the floor, over some newspaper. Mix several colors of poster paints in pie tins. Have your child step in the paint and walk on the sheet, making a footprint tablecloth!

PLACECARD: Use solid-colored paper plates. Write the guests' names on the *underside* of each plate and let the children search for their places.

MENU

Puzzle Punch
Guess What? Sandwich
What's Next? Salad
Clue Cookies

CAKE

Detective's I.D. Cake

ARRIVAL ACTIVITY

Using 3″ x 5″ index cards, make a detective's I.D. card for each child. Put in as much detail as you think the

41

children can handle. As they come to the party, give them a card and a pencil and let them fill in the information. If you have a self-developing camera, it is fun to paste a photo of each guest on the corner of the card. If not, use an ink pad (or a folded paper towel in a dish with poster paint) and have each child put his thumb print in the corner.

ADDITIONAL ACTIVITIES

MYSTERY BOXES: Gather a number of boxes (big enough to accommodate a child's hand) with lids. Put something unusual (a pickle, rubber bands, macaroni, powder puff, etc.) inside each box. Cut a small (hand-size) hole in the end of the boxes. Put a pad of paper and a pencil on top of each box and a basket at the end of the row. Have the children take turns feeling the objects and writing their names and guesses on a slip of paper. Deposit all the guesses in the basket. (Be sure to mark each guess—Box #1, Box #2, etc.). After all the guesses are in, open the boxes and read the guesses. The child with the most correct guesses is dubbed "Super Sleuth."

MYSTERY BALLOONS: Same idea as above, only using balloons instead. Insert small objects in balloons (pennies, popcorn, beans, nuts, buttons, paper clips, etc.). Then blow them up and tie them. Have the children shake each balloon and guess what is inside.

MYSTERY STORY: Ask the children's librarian at your public library to help you select a short mystery story. Read the story aloud to the children, stopping before the story ends. Ask the children to tell, draw or act out an ending.

POLICE SKETCH: Read off a description of a person stating eye color, hair, height, weight, scars, clothing, etc. Have the children each draw their version of the "suspect."

EYEWITNESS REPORT: Have an older brother, sister or friend dress up in a silly outfit (big hat, clashing colors, mismatched shoes, etc.) in a back bedroom. At a designated time, have the "suspect" walk through the party and out the back door. Ask the children to describe what they saw. Be prepared for some conflicting reports!

GAMES

I See Something
Who Am I?
Memory Game

FAVORS

Badges (store-bought or styrofoam*)
Plastic handcuffs and other police
    paraphernalia
Lollipop magnifying glasses (see Decorations)

TAKE HOMES

Staple the sides of a manila folder to make a Detective's Kit. You may wish to add a handle by punching two holes in the tab and running a piece of yarn through. Knot the ends.

*Cut a star from a styrofoam meat tray. Use the whole tray for each star to allow for shrinkage. Color it yellow with a felt marker. Place the badges on foil on a cookie sheet. Bake at 350° for a few minutes, checking often. Remove and let cool a few minutes. Tape a safety pin to the back.

43

THANK YOU

Use inexpensive plain note cards. Print "Guess who says thank you?" on the front. Have your child sign his or her name on the inside.

10

Olympiad

Boy/Girl 7, 8, 9

Even though the Olympics occur only once every four years, sports and competition are always popular, especially with energetic 7, 8 and 9 year olds! You may want to have this party during the summer as an unbirthday for a child with a winter birthday, or to celebrate summer vacation!

This party can be restricted to a sports theme, but our favorite way is to emphasize the countries that are represented in the Olympic games. Not only do the children have fun with the games and activities, but their awareness of other countries' flags, customs and food is brought into the picture. One idea is to assign a nation for each child to represent (via the invitation). He or she then arrives at the party dressed in a costume representing the assigned nation with track clothes underneath! The costumes can be abandoned for the sports events.

INVITATIONS

A folded white piece of paper with the Olympiad insignia and the honoree's name and age on the cover is simple yet effective.

On the inside, you can write in all the party information as well as assign a nation to be represented.

DECORATIONS

The color scheme should correlate with the five colors of the Olympic insignia.

These five colors (blue, yellow, black, green and red) can be carried through with balloons and crepe-paper streamers.

Another decoration idea is to have your child draw and color international flags and attach them to the walls or obtain travel posters from your local travel agency. If they're not willing to give them to you, they may loan them to you.

CENTERPIECE: Using your (or the library's) encyclopedia, draw small flags of the countries you'll have represented. Attach the flags to bamboo skewers and stick them, together with skewered fruit, into a base made of half a head of cabbage.

PLACECARD/PLACE MAT: See Arrival Activity

MENU

Tacos
Tropical fruit spears
Fortune Cookies
Juice Brenner

46

CAKE

Olympiad cake

ARRIVAL ACTIVITY

Have each child draw and color the flag of his or her country using an encyclopedia as a guide. (Some dictionaries also have a page showing various national flags.)

ADDITIONAL ACTIVITY

Parade of Nations: Have children dressed in costumes and holding flags form a parade (as in the Olympic games) with musical background. Let your child be the Torch Bearer, with a paper torch. To make the torch, simply glue a 5½" x 8½" piece of orange tissue paper to the top of an 8½" x 11" piece of construction paper. Roll them into a cone and secure with tape. Twist the top of the tissue paper to resemble a flame.

GAMES

INDOOR/OUTDOOR DECATHLON

Backwards Run
Ball Toss
Bean Bag Toss (with variations)
Book-on-the-Head Race
Frisbee Throw
Hopping
Hop-Skip-Jump
Obstacle Course

Pillowcase Race
Sprints

The winner of each event wins a gold medal.

FAVORS

OLYMPIC GOLD MEDALS: Purchase gold-foil covered chocolate coins and glue on ribbon necklaces.

BADGES: Attach short strips of crepe paper to flattened aluminum foil cupcake cups to resemble prize ribbons. Pin on victors.

TAKE HOMES

A take-home bag really isn't necessary, due to the fact that the children will be excited and proud to wear their medals home to show off.

THANK YOU

As each child leaves for home, he can be handed an uninflated balloon with a "Thank you" message already written on it. For instructions regarding how to write on balloons, see Invitations for "Clowns, Clowns, Clowns."

11

*We are amazed at how many
children want to be hobos on
Hallowe'en . . . so have a Hobo
party any time of the year. The kids
will love it and the moms won't
worry about party clothes.*

Boy/Girl 7, 8, 9

Hobo Hobnob

INVITATIONS

Using a standard-size post card from the post office, glue
patchwork wrapping paper to the information side of the
card. Write out the party information with a bold black
felt-tip pen. Address and mail.

DECORATIONS

Have a sign hanging over or on the front door that reads:
"Welcome to Chris's Hobo Hobnob." If you really want to

create an effect, nail a 1″ x 4″ board at an angle across your front door. The children will get a kick out of crawling through a "condemned building." If you really don't want extra nail holes in your house, use brown mailing paper to simulate boards and tape up.

Interior decorations can be trains, patches, old tin cans and cleaned and decorated garbage cans. This is one party for which you won't feel obligated to clean house!!!

CENTERPIECE: Invert an old hat and place a block of styrofoam inside. Arrange miniknapsacks filled with goodies on skewers in styrofoam.

PLACECARD/PLACE MAT: Cut a brown paper grocery bag into 11″ × 17″ place mat size. Write each guest's name boldly on the place mats. Place a cloth bandana on the side or tuck into a glass. The bandana will then double as a napkin and a knapsack. Or have the children make a Patchwork Place Mat. See Arrival Activity.

MENU

Hot dogs and Beans in tuna cans or
    Meatloafers
Garbage Can Lids

Goldfish crackers (commercial)
Boston Baked Beans Candy in Tins
Tin Can Cupcake
Mudmilk (chocolate milk)

CAKE

Boxcar Cake

COSTUMES

On the invitation, ask each child to come to the party dressed as a hobo. When a child arrives, smear some cocoa on his face for the "hobo-look."

ACTIVITIES

Upon arrival, have each child take a plain white 11″ x 17″ paper place mat, purchased in the paper products section of the grocery store, and glue patches to the place mat. The patches can be made from scraps of wrapping paper or fabric. Have the children rip rather than cut the patches.

GAMES

Gone Fishin' (Go Fish)
Penny Pitch
Scavenger Hunt

FAVORS

Bubble gum cigars
Marbles
Knapsacks
Bubble Pipe (see Peace Pipe Bubbles)

TAKE HOMES

Before the children leave, have them place their favors and prizes in the center of their bandana. Tie the opposite corners together in a knot, then tie them again around a pole. Bring the two remaining ends together and tie twice around the pole. For the pole, buy ¼" doweling at a lumberyard and cut it into desired lengths (approximately 24" each).

THANK YOU

Have your child write out notes of thanks on pieces of paper 4" x 9". Glue these notes around the outside of a 15-oz. empty can to resemble a label. The can can be used at home as a pencil holder.

12

This bicycle party is a fun party to put on from Mom's point of view, and equally enjoyable for the kids. We have two party variations.

Boy/Girl 7, 8, 9

Bike Road-Day-O

Bike Road-Day-O #1

INVITATIONS

Using red construction paper, make a stop-sign-shaped invitation. Use traffic terms to relate party information.

For example: "One Way" to my house, "Merge" on Friday, etc.

Make sure you inform each guest to bring his or her bicycle.

DECORATIONS

The general color scheme is tied in with road sign colors: bright red, green and yellow. Streamers in these colors along with construction paper or poster-board street signs attached to the walls or suspended from the ceiling are effective.

CENTERPIECE: The birthday cake can serve as the centerpiece for this party (see Cake).

TABLECLOTH/PLACECARD: Use a brightly colored red, yellow or green tablecloth. You can dye an old white sheet to arrive at the right color. Using nontoxic felt-tip pens, draw road signs on plain white paper plates.

For placecards, suspend arrows from the ceiling with each guest's name pointing to where he or she will sit.

MENU

Pizza Wheels
Orange-up Float
Antipasto

CAKE

Stop Sign Cake or red, yellow and green frosted cupcakes

COSTUMES

You may choose to have each guest arrive in a costume of his or her theme choice.

ARRIVAL ACTIVITY

As each guest arrives, direct him or her to an area where you have placed playing cards, clothespins, balloons, crepe paper, plastic flowers, berry baskets, yarn, old shoes, tin cans, ribbons, bows, tin foil and masking tape. Let each child decorate his or her bicycle as desired.

ADDITIONAL ACTIVITY

You may wish to invite a representative from your local police department to come to your home and give a bicycle safety inspection, a lecture on bicycle rules or set up an obstacle course.

GAMES

Red Light, Green Light
Bicycle Obstacle Course

FAVORS

- Safety flags for bicycles can be obtained from large discount stores, bicycle shops or automotive shops. You may want to personalize this favor by writing each child's name on his flag.
- Bicycle safety pamphlets obtained from your local police or fire department.
- For the super-industrious mother, try backpacks made

of cloth (patterns can be found at fabric shops), given to each child to put his or her name on in crayon and then ironed (see "Birthday Parties for Toddlers").

• Bicycle reflectors purchased from a large discount store, bicycle shop or automotive store.

TAKE HOMES

Homemade backpacks (see Favors).

THANK YOU

Cut a circle of poster board about 5″ in diameter and color the edge black to resemble a bicycle tire. On one side have your child write a thank you message. On the other side write mailing information. Stamp and mail. (You may have to put more postage on it than on an ordinary post card. Call your postmaster for details.)

Bike Road-Day-O #2

This party follows the same outline as our above-mentioned party. The difference is that after all the guests have arrived and decorated their bikes, they go on a bike hike to a nearby park or other recreational facility. (Be sure all the parents approve.)

Pack a box lunch (using a shoe box) for each guest consisting of a sandwich, a piece of fruit and an individual container of milk or fruit juice.

You may wish to have the children decorate these shoe-box containers as an opening activity. Provide yarn, paper, magazines, ribbons, flowers, etc. if you choose this option.

This is a good outing for both Dad and Mom to attend, or a "helper chaperone." Set a specific time for the children to return for cake and celebrations.

One of our favorite pastimes as little girls was "dress-up." If your little girl likes to be like Mommy, this party will fulfill all her fantasies. Ask the guests to come dressed for a "grown-up" party. You'll be delighted to see the girls rise to the occasion and act like little ladies.

This is a very formal luncheon that, of course, needs to be served by a maid and butler (Mommy and Daddy). Wear a black dress and white apron. Make a collar and cap with white paper. Have Daddy dress in his best dark suit and white shirt. You may even be able to talk big brother into playing busboy. Oh, how special your daughter will feel!

Girls 7, 8, 9

Tea Party

INVITATIONS

A formal luncheon requires formal invitations. Buy plain, solid-colored (pink or white is nice) note cards and write the standard:

58

Miss Kacey Barron
Requests the pleasure of your company
for luncheon
Saturday, December 29, at Noon

DECORATIONS

Decorate your home the way you would if you were having the luncheon for your friends. Set the table with your nicest tablecloth (a flowered sheet will do). Use your best china and silver. (Remember, if you treat them as ladies, they will act that way!) Put a big bowl or basket of fresh flowers in the center of the table.

PLACECARD: Use cloth napkins. If you don't have any, buy a remnant of nice cotton and rip it in desired sizes. Then pull a few threads on each edge to fray. Roll each napkin and tie with a ribbon. Write each guest's name on a small card and punch a hole in the corner. Slip it on the ribbon like a gift tag, add a flower and tie a bow.

MENU

Pretty as a Princess Puffs
Sunshine Salad
Sweet Tea or Mocha Flip
Parfaits

CAKE

Hazelnut Torte or Petit Fours

ACTIVITIES

MAKE A PURSE. Cut a round (circle) of fabric 10″ in diameter. Using a hole puncher, punch holes 1″ in from the edges and about 1″ apart. (Yes, a hole puncher works on fabric . . . we were amazed.) Lace a 12″ shoestring or ribbon through the holes and draw together.

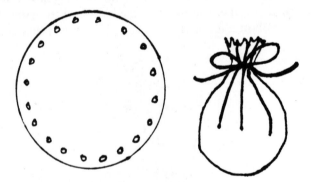

BEAUTY PARLOR. Set up some mirrors. Fill baskets with hair brushes, combs, curlers, make-up, ribbons, barrettes and let the girls take turns making each other up.

GAMES

Drop the Hankie (Duck, Duck, Goose)
Telephone
Bring the Princess a Gift

FAVORS

Play make-up
Barrettes
Curlers
Ribbons
Brushes
Combs
Paper dolls

TAKE HOMES

Make a "shopping bag" for the girls to take home. Use a
large grocery bag, or make one out of pretty gift wrap and
add yarn handles. Write the birthday child's name on the
side. For example: "Betsy's Boutique."

THANK YOU

Buy some pretty, flowered note cards and write a formal
thank you.

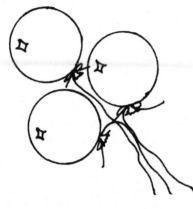

Holiday Parties

Holidays are to be celebrated, and what better way than with a party? There are other reasons, too, for choosing a holiday theme for a party.

A birthday near a holiday is often overshadowed by the holiday. We have mentioned that we each have a child with a December 29th birthday. Trying to collect steam to throw a dynamite party when we haven't finished picking up the wrapping papers from the Christmas presents has been a nearly impossible endeavor over the years. By the time Sam reached five, he was in agreement that he didn't need any more presents, especially after the Christmas deluge. To Sam a June 29th party sounded like loads of fun. On the other hand, Kacey, age 4, wasn't ready to make that concession! It's important to talk over a date change with your child and gain his or her agreement as well as enthusiasm. After all, it is *the child's* special day.

The weather may be a factor for choosing a holiday

party. A child with a wintertime birthday may wish to exchange a cold-weather party for a sunny swimming party—and vice versa.

You may have relatives who only come to visit during holidays and never have a chance to be present for the celebration of your child's birthday. A remedy would be to tie the two together with a holiday party. Grandparents especially get a new thrill from seeing their "angels" interplay with their young friends.

If you are having children (cousins, for instance) as holiday or vacation house guests for a lengthy period of time, let them plan and prepare for a party. It may get them out of your hair for awhile, too!

On Hallowe'en, many parents are apprehensive about letting their young ones out on the streets for safety reasons. Hallowe'en parties are a very acceptable substitute for trick-or-treating.

No matter what the reason, the giving of a holiday party can be an enjoyable experience for you and your child.

Please note: For a St. Valentine's Day party, refer to "Hearts Galore," and for a Thanksgiving party, see "Pow-Wow."

St. Patrick's Day Party

INVITATIONS

Draw a shamrock shape on the bottom half of an 8½″ x 11″ piece of green construction paper. Inside the shamrock, print the party information. Fold the paper in half, attach with a sticker or staple, address and mail. (Be sure to tell the invitee to wear green!)

DECORATIONS

Go crazy with the color green! Use green streamers, balloons, tablecloth, plates and cups.

MENU

Lucky Leprechauns (see Teatime
Sandwiches)
Irish Milk (add green food coloring to milk)
Celery sticks
Shamrock Sandies (see Ice Cream Sandies
   and use shamrock-shaped sugar cookies
   and green ice cream)

ACTIVITY

LUCKY CHARM NECKLACES: These lucky charm necklaces are very easy to make. Before the party, cut shamrock shapes from 3″ squares of green construction paper. Each child will need twelve shamrocks. On both the left and the right leaves of each shamrock, punch a hole. Cut a 42″ piece of green or white yarn for each child. When the children arrive, have them lace the yarn through the shamrocks (in the left hole, out the right). If the yarn ends get frazzled, wrap a tiny bit of clear plastic tape around the tip. After all twelve shamrocks have been laced, tie the ends together to make a necklace.

GAMES

I Spy the Leprechaun
Penny Hunt
Musical Shamrocks (see Musical Hearts)

Easter Egg Party

INVITATIONS

This Easter basket carries a very important message.

Cut twice as many 3″ x 5″ pieces from brown construction paper or grocery bags as you will have guests. Use two pieces for each basket. Glue the edges together on both sides and the bottom. Attach a 1″ x 6″ strip of brown paper as a handle. Cut five 2″ long egg shapes from various spring colors of construction paper for each basket. Put part of the party information on each egg and place in the basket. For mailing, tuck the handle inside the basket, place in a standard-size envelope, address and mail.

DECORATIONS

For each child, cut an egg-shaped place mat from an 11″ x 14″ piece of colored construction paper. Have your child decorate each place mat and put aside until the party.

For a centerpiece, use a large basket tied with a fancy ribbon bow. Inside the basket, shred green sheet crepe paper to resemble grass. Place eggs inside the basket.

MENU

Gelatin Eggs
Easter Egg Sandies (egg salad in quartered
   pocket pita bread)
Bunny Food (celery, carrots and raisins in
   miniature party baskets found at dime
   stores)
Cupcake Baskets
Yogurt shakes

ACTIVITIES

EGG DECORATING: For egg decorating, use hard-boiled eggs and commercial egg-decorating kits from your local grocery store. Follow the directions found on the kit's package.

EGG HUNT: Hide the eggs before the party (depending on the weather, the hunt may have to be indoors. If this is the case, make sure you count the number of eggs hidden. A hard-boiled egg lost for weeks doesn't emit a pleasant scent!) You may choose to use plastic eggs that can be filled with coins, candy, small novelties or slips of paper with activities to perform written on them (i.e., "Hop 5 times"). Be sure to gear the activities to the age level. These plastic eggs can be purchased at the grocery store or dime store.

EASTER BASKETS FOR VERY ORGANIZED MOTHERS: About a month before the party, start buying your milk in quart-size containers. Save these empty cleaned cartons until you have enough to provide one for each child. Or, if your child is school age, have him bring home individual-size (half-pint) milk containers. A good scavenger might be able to bring home enough the first day! Cut the carton down so that it is 2″ deep. Now cut a 2″-wide piece of lightly colored construction paper to wrap around the outside of the carton. Cut it to fit and staple it to the carton.

Two weeks before the party, cut 1″-thick kitchen sponges to fit into the bottom of each carton. Moisten sponge and sprinkle a handful of grass seed (from your local nursery) or bird seed (believe it or not!) over the sponge. Have your child sprinkle each basket daily with enough water to keep it continually moist. Place containers in a sunny window sill. By the day of the party, each container should have sprouted beautiful green grass. You might make a couple of extras just in case Mother Nature randomly fails to produce! Hide jelly beans in this grass. When the children arrive, they can each decorate the outside of these containers with marking pens.

GAMES

Egg Toss
Egg-'n-Spoon Relay
Mystery Egg

All-American Jamboree
(Flag Day, July 4th, Veterans' Day)

INVITATIONS

Cut an 8½″ x 11″ piece of red construction paper in half lengthwise. Use one half per invitation. Round each end to resemble a firecracker. Poke one half of a white pipe cleaner near the top (to resemble a fuse) and secure it with tape on the back. Write your party particulars on the front. Fold the pipe cleaner down, fold the paper in half, staple, address and mail (see diagram).

DECORATIONS

This will probably be a summertime party (July 4th), so we suggest you take it to a park. Cover the tables with newsprint (see Backyard Mural, p. 121) and run twisted red, white and blue streamers down the center of the table. Be sure to tape the paper and streamers underneath. If it is likely to be windy, use thumbtacks. Use the Flag Cake (see below) for the centerpiece.

Wrap each guest's utensils in a solid-colored napkin (red, white or blue) and tie with curling ribbon. Curl the ends and place an American flag toothpick in each bow. These miniature flags are usually available by the package in most party goods sections of your favorite variety store.

MENU

Yipes Stripes Gelatin
Blueberry Pancake Rolls (see Pancake Rolls)
Strawberries or cherry tomatoes
Patriotic Punch (see O.J. "Sip"-Son)
Flag Cake

ACTIVITIES

PAPER HATS: Let's have a parade! As the guests arrive, seat them at a table to decorate a parade hat. You may want to fold these paper hats ahead of time or have the children fold them at the party. Use newspaper, newsprint or large 11" x 14" construction paper. Supply the troops with red and blue crayons, marking pens, gummed stars, flag stickers and red and blue plastic tape (see diagram).

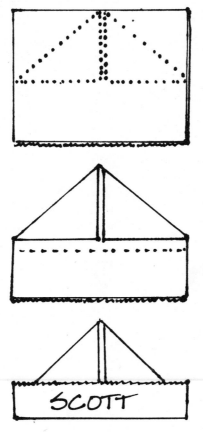

MUSICAL INSTRUMENTS: When the hats are complete, give each child a musical instrument. Again, depending on your age group and time frame, make the instruments ahead of time or have the children make them.

> Drum (see Pow-Wow)
> Shaker (see Pow-Wow)
> Tin cans (beat two together)
> Bells
> Spoons (two together and back-to-back)
> Sand blocks (cover two wooden blocks with sandpaper)
> Pot lids
> Aluminum pot and a wooden spoon

Now you are ready for a "Spirit of '76" march around the block!

Hallowe'en

INVITATIONS

Cut 8½" x 11" pieces of white construction paper in half to get one 4¼" x 11" piece per guest. From each piece cut a long ghost shape. Print the party information, fold, place in an envelope, address and mail (see diagram).

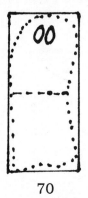

DECORATIONS

Acquire one very large pumpkin to use as a table center-piece. Instead of carving this pumpkin, decorate it with fruits and vegetables! Use toothpicks as the fasteners. A half of a bell pepper, either red or green, can be used for each of the ears. An Italian green pepper makes a nose like no other. A mouth can be made of raisins all in a row. Just open your refrigerator and use your imagination. Top it all with a floppy straw hat or one of your choice. The children will love it.

Orange and black crepe-paper streamers along with construction paper witches' hats, ghosts, pumpkins and cats suspended from the ceiling will contribute to that already-excited feeling that young children have at Hallowe'en time.

MENU

Pumpkin Sand-Witches
Witches' Brew
Bobbin apples
Roasted pumpkin seeds
Orange-up
Jack-o-Lantern Cake

ACTIVITIES

PUMPKIN HUNT: Take the children to a local pumpkin patch to choose their very own Hallowe'en pumpkin. Depending on the number of children, you might need to have an additional adult for driving. Nevertheless, it can be such a thrilling experience for the children that a little extra organization isn't so bad. Make sure you call ahead of time to verify that the patch will be open to visitors. Also, if they know you're coming with a group, they might give you some special treatment. Find out the cost per pound and decide on just how much can be spent for each pumpkin. Find the size that will serve as a model. The child can match the model to the one he has chosen and know before picking whether or not his pumpkin is an acceptable size. You'll find that most children aren't as concerned about a pumpkin's size as they are its character. Don't hesitate to get right in there with them. All children love to have adults mix with them. Besides, who said you can't enjoy the party, too!

As each pumpkin is chosen, mark the bottom of it with the child's initials.

If you don't have a real pumpkin patch in your area, don't fret. Many urban areas have vegetable stands that load up on pumpkins for Hallowe'en. Take your gang to one of these, or go to the grocery store and purchase as many small, irregular-shaped pumpkins as you will have children. You can hide them in your home, in your yard, or even in a few neighbors' yards. Don't forget to alert your neighbors in case you choose the latter!

PUMPKIN SEED ROAST: After the hunt, return home for the roasting of pumpkin seeds (use the "key" pumpkin for the seeds and the recipe in the recipe chapter of this book), an apple bob (see Games) and a warming meal.

Christmas Party

INVITATIONS

This snowflake invitation can double as a tree ornament. Fold a 6″ x 6″ piece of white paper in half and then half again. Cut small triangle shapes around the edges and in the middle. Unfold to find a snowflake! Punch a hole in one corner and tie a string through it. Write the party information on the uncut areas of the paper. Place in an envelope, stamp, address and mail.

DECORATIONS

You will probably have your holiday decorations and tree up by the time of the party. No additional decorations should be necessary.

MENU

Razzamatazz
Cream cheese stuffed celery
Cherry tomatoes
Cheese crêpes (see Crêpes for Kids)
Snowballs

ACTIVITIES

COOKIE DECORATING: Before the party, you and your child can make up a couple of batches of our sugar cookie recipe. Use Christmas cookie cutters. Just before the children arrive, make up various colors of frosting. A quick and easy way to do this is to purchase a can of prepared white frosting. Divide the frosting into separate bowls. Add a different color of food coloring to each bowl of frosting and mix well. Or mix powdered sugar, water and food coloring in small jars until you reach paint consistency. Put a small paint brush in each jar. Supply the children with a plate of cookies apiece and let them go to town!

73

RUDOLPH PLAY: While the cookies are drying, hand out the "Rudolph Play" costumes for rehearsal. Before you panic at the thought of making eight reindeer costumes as well as a Santa costume, relax. Each costume is simply a construction paper headband. You will need one piece of 11" x 14" brown construction paper per guest, plus one piece each of red and white 11" x 14" construction paper.

Cut the reindeer hats as shown in the diagram. Put a hole on either end of the band and tie an 8" -piece of yarn through each hole. Make one Santa hat in the same manner, gluing the white paper on the red. Cut a red circle for Rudolph's nose. Punch two holes and tie 12" strings to each.

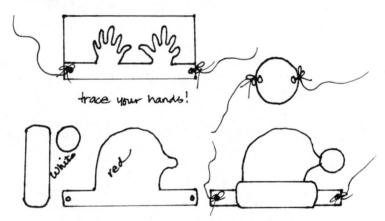

trace your hands!

white   red

Now it's time to play or sing "Rudolph the Red Nose Reindeer" for the children. Ask them to listen carefully, then tell you what it means. Next, let the children choose the parts of Santa Claus, Rudolph and the reindeer. Be sure to tell them they'll each get a turn to play the "lead." Now they can act out the story. The story pretty well tells itself, but you may wish to "direct" a little.

Go over your play several times, letting everyone get a chance to be Santa and/or Rudolph. By this time,

74

the children should be able to sing the song without your help, and you're ready to take your act out on the road!

Instead of having the children's parents pick them up, arrange to drive each child home. Make your first stop a convalescent hospital or retirement center. (Arrange with the institution in advance.) The children can perform their rendition of "Rudolph" for this very appreciative audience, and share their decorated cookies. Bring a handkerchief, as this experience will lend itself to some poignant moments. It could even turn into an annual event!

CHRISTMAS WALL HANGING: Cut as many 11″ x 14″ pieces of white burlap as you will have children. You can purchase burlap at your local fabric store. Mix a medium-size bowl of green poster paint and a small bowl of red poster paint. Place newspaper under the burlap piece. Have each child dip his hand into the green paint and then blot it on the burlap with fingers pointing outward six times in order to form a wreath shape. Dip the thumb of the child's clean hand in the red paint and have him blot his thumbprint between the handprints to resemble holly berries. Set the painting aside to dry and wash the child's hands. Repeat this procedure until each child has completed his Christmas wall hanging.

ORNAMENTS: On a table covered with waxed paper, supply the children with a variety of shapes of pretzels and with white glue. While they are gluing ornament shapes, make up cans of brightly colored poster paints mixed with enough liquid starch to make a semithick consistency.

When the glued pretzels are dry, have the children dip these pretzels into the poster paint mixture. Use a paper clip, partially unfolded, as a dipping utensil. Hang painted pretzels on a clothes line to dry in an area where they will not be bothered. (Cover the floor under the line with newspaper to catch any paint drips.)

Special Parties for Special Kids

As the parent of a special child, you are constantly reminded that your child is different, and who needs that? Everybody has a birthday and everybody loves a party. Exceptional children are no exception!

It is very tempting to send some cupcakes to school and let it go at that. But your child probably goes to school out of your neighborhood and rarely gets a chance to entertain at home. So be brave and have a real party!

Now, we said be brave, not a martyr. You're going to need some help. Neighbors, relatives and friends are a good source, but your best bet is your child's teacher. Most special education teachers and aides are the type of people who would love to come to your home for a party. It gives them a chance to see the children in a different environment where the object is fun.

You will probably want to invite your child's classmates. Most special education classes are small, so go ahead and invite the whole class. It avoids any hurt feelings. Don't be afraid to include nonhandicapped children. Special friends from the neighborhood will add new faces for children who have the same classmates year in and year out. It will be a big help to you and an enriching experience for all.

You know your child very well, but all children are different. Be sure to check with the parents of the guests for any of their idiosyncrasies. *Ask about toilet habits, medications and seizures.*

Check with the teacher for some general suggestions. He or she will be a good resource.

Look through our theme parties and see if one of them appeals to you and your child. If you don't wish to adapt one of ours, choose your child's favorite cartoon character, movie or pet and carry that theme through the party.

Here we offer some suggestions for various handicaps.

Physically Handicapped

Your child may not be in a wheelchair, but his friends may be, so be prepared! Be aware of architectural barriers. If it's a nice day, have the party outdoors; if it is not, you might try decorating your garage.

If you have the party in your family room, move some furniture out to the garage . . . you'll need lots of room. Borrow a large piece of plywood or a couple of 1' × 4's for a wheelchair ramp.

If the children are heavy and nonambulatory, make sure you have some strong men on hand to help with toileting.

Make your party colorful and festive. Have some crepe-paper streamers and balloons on hand to decorate the wheelchairs and crutches. Place the children in a circle for eating and activities.

If you have the energy, make a workboard for each guest as a special party favor. Buy a sheet of plywood at a lumber yard and have it cut to your specifications (12″ × 13″ is probably best). Sand the edges and paint or stain. Use stick-on letters (available at hardware or hobby stores) to spell each child's name. Complete the board with colorful decals or glued felt shapes, rick rack, pictures, etc. The boards will be useful during the party as well as a nice change of pace for the children to have at home and school.

GAMES

What Am I?
Who Am I?
Secret Word Story
I See Something
Go Fish
Bean Bag
Pin-the-Nose-on-the _____
Space Flight
Simon Says
Hot Potato
Musical Chairs (chalk circles on patio or
    driveway)
Spelling Scramble
Wink-Wink

ACTIVITIES

Play-Dough and Dough-Art
Printing
Pretzels
Bean bags

79

Puppets
Finger painting
Rock art
Fruit Face
Peace Pipe Bubbles

Developmentally Disabled
(Mentally Retarded)

Most of our theme parties can easily be adapted to the developmentally disabled child. But you will probably want to keep the party as simple as possible. Give the children lots of leeway. Take their attention span into account. Not all your ideas will go as planned, so be prepared just to let the children have free play. Have a basket of "shareable" toys on hand.

Don't be afraid to plan some games, but keep them short and sweet. Gear the games and activities to your child, but be prepared for a wide range of personalities and capabilities. Save an extra helping of patience for the day of the party—you'll need it! Keep in mind that the children are not stubborn, per se, but just have difficulty switching channels!

Zero your efforts in on your menu. It is sure to be the highlight of the party. Read our menu ideas to your child and let her or him choose the favorites. It may not be what you would have chosen, but it will be what the child will enjoy—and eat!

We offer the following suggestions for games and activities:

GAMES

Decathlon
Musical Chairs
Duck, Duck, Goose

What Am I?
Animal Races
Rain Dance
Red Light, Green Light (on foot)
Secret Word Story Time
Sponge Bowling
Balloon games
Bean Bags
Copy Cat Dance
Go Fish
Pin-the-?-on-the-_____
Shoe Race
Penny Hunt
Footprint Folly

ACTIVITIES

Play-Dough and Dough-Art
Puppets (made ahead of time for favors)
Finger painting
Peace Pipe Bubbles

Deaf and Hard of Hearing

You and your child should sit down and plan the party together. What a marvelous language experience for you both to share! If your child uses Total Communication, be sure to invite someone else who signs to help you. Decide ahead of time how you will explain the games and activities in case you need to look up any new signs.

Many inexpensive favors are available through N.A.D. (National Association of the Deaf, 814 Thayer Avenue, Silver Springs, Maryland 20910). Also, you may wish to borrow or rent (from a camera shop) a movie projector and send away for a captioned film (Captioned

81

Films, Inc., 624 E. Walnut Street, Suite 223, Indian-
apolis, Indiana 46204). Otherwise, we recommend the
following:

GAMES

Decathlon
Obstacle Course
Duck, Duck, Goose
Animal Races
Red Light, Green Light (make signs for "it" to
   hold)
Sponge Bowling
Balloon games
Bean Bag activities
Drop the Clothespin
Copy Cat Dance
Pass the Apple
Twister
Go Fish
Penny Pitch
Pin-the-?-on-the-_____
Shoe Race
Space Flight
Penny Hunt
Sandbox Search
Apple Bob
Button-Button
Footprint Folly
Follow that String
Egg Toes

ACTIVITIES

Play-Dough and Dough-Art
Printing activities

Pretzels
Puppets
Finger painting
Rock art
Fruit Face
Peace Pipe Bubbles

Blind and Visually Handicapped

If your child goes to a neighborhood school (as opposed to a school for the blind), this is a marvelous opportunity to seek out some new friends. Check with your child's counselor or therapist for the names of some other blind children your child's age. Or you may wish to invite all his sighted friends. Plan a simple party (see Traditional Party, page 13), with emphasis on good food and enjoyable games.

Make special placecards for the children and hang them on the backs of the chairs. Either cut the names out of sandpaper and glue on smooth cardboard or write the names in glue and sprinkle with sand or glitter. A good variation is to write with honey (using a squeeze bottle) and sprinkle with sugar.

A special surprise for the children is to tape record the party and play it back just as the children are leaving.

GAMES

Animal Races (parents position the children)
Pillowcase Hop (see Indoor/Outdoor
    Decathlon)
Book-on-the-Head Race (see
    Indoor/Outdoor Decathlon)
Rain Dance

Red Light, Green Light (with parent)
Secret Word Story
Pass the Apple
Go Fish
Ring the Bell (see Bean Bags)
Apple Bob
Mother May I (no cheating)
Follow that String
Mystery Person

Multi-Handicapped

A birthday is special even for the very severely handicapped child. This is a beautiful opportunity to show your special child off. An appealing hat and colorful balloons may be all you need. Ask for extra long strings on your helium balloons and tie them to your guests' hands, arms or legs, or put a bell inside the balloons before you inflate them.

Peace Pipe Bubbles (page 126) are fun for Mothers to blow. Also, the children will probably enjoy a little music.

Look through our recipe ideas for some good "feelies." The yogurt snacks are usually a hit. You'll need lots of help at feeding time, so plan a one-to-one ratio of helpers to children.

GAMES

Peace Pipe Bubbles (blow at)
Read a Story
Balloons with long Strings
Chapeau Charades
Go Fish

84

Ring the Bell (see Bean Bags)
Balloon Surprise (bells)

Remember, no matter what your child's handicap, no matter how simple your party, your child's birthday will be yours to treasure together always.

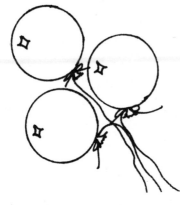

16

Additional Parties

Here are more suggestions on how to have a special party. These do not involve such elaborate preparations as the theme parties but will still be a hit with the children. Let your child look through and pick out a favorite.

Read through the theme parties for planning suggestions such as table settings, decorations, etc., and use the recipe suggestions for menu ideas.

BACKWARDS PARTY

Start by writing your invitations backwards and ask all your guests to dress backwards. At the party, serve all the food backwards (cake and ice cream *before* lunch—the kids will love it!) Tell the children to walk backwards; spell their names on the placecards backwards, etc. It's great fun and a real challenge.

KITE PARTY

This is a good idea for an early spring, late winter party. Buy an inexpensive kite for each guest, and a couple of extras for emergencies, and let them all have fun putting them together. Cut long strips of colorful cloth and put them in a basket. Let each child choose his or her favorites to make a tail. Also offer felt pens so the children can decorate and personalize their kites.

After lunch and a kite-shaped cake, walk the kids to a nice open area and, "Go fly a kite!"

FAIRY TALE PARTY

Choose your child's favorite fairy tale or book and carry out the theme. Have your girl be the fairy princess, complete with a tinfoil crown* and magic wand, or your son be the prince—or the monster! Read the children the theme fairy tale or have them act it out.

TEE SHIRT PARTY

Cut a tee-shirt shape from a piece of white construction paper for your invitation. Ask your guests to bring a plain white tee shirt (or if you feel you can swing it, buy a couple of packages of them at a discount store). Give the children crayons (see page 9), permanent felt markers, iron-on patches, etc. and let them decorate their own tee shirts. If your child enjoys sewing, offer needles and thread with a variety of lace, rick rack, sequins, etc. Have a "fashion show" and finish with a Tee-Shirt Cake.

---

*Or an inexpensive dime-store chiffon scarf tucked in the top of a cone-shaped party hat will turn your little girl into a "fair damsel."

MARCHING BAND PARTY

Ask your guests to bring a musical instrument (home-made or otherwise!). Have the children make hats (see "Clowns, Clowns, Clowns") and pin some gold braid and fringe (from a yardage store) to their shoulders. Let your child be the drum major and have a parade up and down your street. Serve a Drum Cake. See "All-American Jamboree" for additional instrument ideas.

DOLL PARTY

Write the invitations on cut-out paper dolls (see "Hearts Galore"). Asks guests to bring their favorite dolls. Offer doll clothes, baby bottles, diapers (little squares of flannel) as favors and prizes. Have a make-believe meal for the dolls and serve a Doll Carriage Cake. Pin placecards to the tablecloth with diaper pins.

RAH-RAH, SIS BOOM BAH! PARTY

Ask guests to come dressed in their favorite team's colors. Make your invitations in the shape of a pennant. Make crepe-paper pompons as favors. Divide the guests into teams and have a cheerleading competition.

ICE CREAM SOCIAL

You may wish to have your party in a local ice cream parlor, or you may wish to have the ice cream parlor in your own home! Buy some inexpensive pink-and-white striped fabric for a tablecloth. Fill a big (preferably clear glass) bowl with scoops of ice cream. Have a variety of sauces available, as well as nuts, fruit, sprinkle candy and, of course, whipped cream. Let each guest make his own or let Daddy dress up as a "soda jerk" and serve.

RECORD HOP

Write your invitations in chalk on black, record shaped construction paper. Ask your guests to each bring a favorite record. Set up your record player (perhaps in the garage), and let the guests teach each other the latest dances.

Bake your cake in a tube pan and frost with dark chocolate frosting. Decorate it as a record with your child's name on the label.

NATURE HIKE

Ask each guest to wear good walking shoes or boots and bring a backpack. Have them meet at your house and fill each back pack with a lunch. (See recipes for trail mix and other goodies.) Pile the kids in the car (or borrow a pick-up) and go somewhere for a nice hike. Organize a "natural scavenger hunt" where the kids look for "2 acorns, 5 white rocks, 2 pine cones," etc. Bring them back to your house after lunch for ice cream and cake.

NOSTALGIA PARTY

Pick an era that appeals to your child (50s, 60s, 70s) and carry the theme through the party. Have the children dress in fashions from that era and play appropriate music. Call the library if you have trouble finding the records you want. Be sure to join in the fun and dress up, too!

COME-AS-YOU-ARE PARTY

There are two ways to do a come-as-you-are party. One way is to telephone your invitations, and the guests come to the party wearing what they are wearing when you call. Make your calls when you think you can catch them in their pajamas or swim suits, etc.

The other way is to prearrange the time and date with your guests' parents and just drive around and pick the children up for a party that's a surprise.

PICNIC IN THE PARK

If it's a nice day, have your party in a nearby park. Ask the guests to come directly there. Go ahead of time to select a good spot and cover the tables with cloths from home. Tie helium balloons to the benches so your guests will spot you easily. Bring frisbees, balls, ropes, etc. for after-lunch fun. (Check with your local parks and recreation department for equipment to borrow.)

90

SLUMBER PARTY

Ask guests to bring sleeping bags, pajamas and their favorite teddy bear. Have them come after dinner and serve a midnight breakfast (see Breakfast Party for menu suggestions). Don't plan on getting any sleep. If you do get a little, it will be a delightful surprise.

PUPPET PARTY

Have the children bring puppets or make puppets at the party (see "Activities"). Make a stage (see "Activities") and have a puppet show. Plan a song or a poem to perform for the kids to break the ice.

BOWLING PARTY

Take all the children to a bowling alley. Call ahead and check on group rates. Bring them back to your house afterwards for ice cream and cake. Bake a sheet cake and decorate it with bowling-pin cookies and jawbreaker bowling balls. For bowling-pin shaped cookies, use a knife to cut the shape and a decorating tube to make red stripes on the neck. Stand the cookies up on the frosted cake.

MINIATURE GOLF PARTY

Ask your guests to meet you at a miniature golf course. Remember to check ahead concerning group discount rates. Come back to your house for a special golf course cake. Bake a sheet cake and frost it with bright green frosting. Sprinkle all the cake except "the green" with green coconut. Glue a little flag to a toothpick and put it in the middle of "the green." Write your birthday or party message on the flag.

SOMEONE'S-IN-THE-KITCHEN-WITH . . . PARTY

Have your birthday child choose a menu that he or she and the guests will prepare themselves and then eat. Sit down with your child beforehand to plan the menu and needed ingredients. Set up these ingredients, recipes and necessary utensils in the kitchen. Then let the kids "go to it!" Your job is to set the table and act as an on-the-spot helper. Don't intervene unless solicited!

BREAKFAST PARTY

Invite your guests to come for breakfast. Suspend doughnuts from the ceiling tied with colorful ribbons and each guest's name for a unique decoration idea as well as bobbing game. A menu idea that's fun is a waffle or pancake smorgasbord. Provide a standard batter to which children may add variations (i.e., apple, chocolate, pineapple, etc.). Provide an array of toppings. Syrup, jams, jellies, whipped cream, sliced fruits, powdered sugar and applesauce are some suggestions.

TALENT SHOW

Make your garage into a stage area using the garage door as a "curtain." Ask each guest to come prepared to perform his or her talent. After the show, hold a "cast party" with cake and ice cream. Decorate the garage with Hollywood-type posters, pass out programs and don't forget the "stage hook"!

CLASH PARTY

Ask guests to wear the wildest combinations of clothing they can come up with. Give prizes to everyone for costumes: one for originality, one for wildest colors, one for funniest, etc. Decorate the cake with "chartreuse" and "lavender" frosting highlighted with reds or blues.

HOME MOVIE PARTY

If you don't own a home movie camera, you can rent one from a camera shop at a minimal expense. Have the children put on a performance. It can be a mime, a song and dance, or a short silent movie. Whatever it is, get it on film. Have the birthday child be the director, complete with beret and megaphone. You can show the movie on another occasion.

An alternative is to ask each guest to bring a favorite home movie to share at the party. Old baby movies will really get funny reactions from the kids. Again, if you don't have a projector, one can be easily rented.

WHEN THE CIRCUS COMES TO TOWN

Periodically, special attractions such as the circus, rodeo or a fair may come to your area. If the event coincides with your child's birthday, you may want to take a special friend or two along for a day's outing. The Chamber of Commerce is a good source for information as to what events are scheduled. Also they may have information on group rates.

BIRTHDAY BARBECUE

If you are fortunate enough to have pleasant weather for your child's birthday, why not have an outdoor barbecue? Dad can be the chef, or the birthday child may wish to try a hand at being chef, or the guests could cook-it-themselves. Try some ideas like kabobs (beef, lamb or chicken), barbecued ribs, or the traditional hot dogs and hamburgers. For a dessert see our recipe for Chocolate Toasties.

FAVORITE FILM PARTY

Build the theme of your child's party around his or her favorite movie or television program. Write to the network that carries the program for addresses for obtaining souvenirs, autographs, posters, etc. It takes some time to get an answer, so plan ahead. Use these for decorations. Some children's books and magazines have addresses for obtaining pictures and posters, too.

LET'S GO TO THE SHOW

An outing kids enjoy is going to a movie in a large group. You pick up all the guests and give each one a goodie bag filled with nutritious treats. Try canned juices as opposed to pops, and snack cakes, cookies and trail mix instead of candy. A special treat is to give each child a *little* pocket money so he or she can be a little frivolous!

If nothing exciting is playing at your local theaters, try the public library. They have films to loan. Rent a movie projector and show the movie in your home "theater." Don't forget the popcorn!

94

TAKE ME OUT TO THE BALL GAME

A good group outing is to take your birthday child and a few friends to a professional ball game, if you are fortunate enough to live in an area where a big game isn't too far away. If you can't make a pro game, try a college or even a high school game. The fanfare is always exciting to a youngster. Mom's duty is to keep the supplies rolling: Make sure that nobody is without food or drink. Dad's job is to keep the enthusiasm up and to explain game rules and regulations.

A-SKATING WE WILL GO

Take your child and friends to a nearby roller skating or ice skating arena. Make sure each child has enough money for skate rental and a treat. You may wish to bring your own party food, such as lunch or cake and ice cream.

SWIMMING PARTY

This party doesn't necessarily have to be in the summertime, as lots of areas have public indoor swimming pools sponsored by local colleges or the YM/YWCA. It also doesn't necessarily have to be a pool. Backyard sprinklers, wading pools, etc. can fit the bill. If you do go to a pool, it is imperative that you assess each child's swimming ability, and that you have *more* than enough qualified supervisors. *NEVER LEAVE CHILDREN ALONE NEAR WATER.*

95

SNOW TRIP

A trip to the snow can be an enjoyable special event if proper preparations are made. Make sure that each child brings at least one change of warm clothing. Pack hearty food like chili beans or beef stew in large thermoses, lots of sandwiches, and hot cocoa. A cake with "coconut snow" would be a delightful extra. Remember that cool weather increases appetites.

17

Games

(alphabetically listed with suggested ages)

97

Mystery Egg   4–9

Mystery Person   7–9

Pass the Apple   8–9

Penny Hunt   3–9

Penny Pitch   4–9

Pin the . . .   4–9

Rain Dance   3–6

Red Light, Green
   Light   4–9

Sandbox Search   3–6

Scavenger Hunt   7–9

Secret Word Story
   Time   7–9

Shoe Race   4–6

Simon Says   4–9

Space Flight   6–9

Spelling Scramble   7–9

Sponge Bowling   3–6

Telephone   4–9

Treasure Hunt   8–9

Twister   8–9

Watch Where You Sit   4–9

What Am I?   3–9

Who Am I?   6–9

Wink, Wink   8–9

ANIMAL RACES

Have children race from one point to another using the following styles:

BUNNY HOP: Child must hop from starting point to finish line.

CRAB WALK: Child walks on hands and feet, tummy up.

DUCK WALK: Child walks with hands tucked in underarms while in a squatting position.

LEAP FROG: Team competition. One child gets down on hands and knees while the second child leaps over him or her. Positions are then alternated until the goal is reached.

APPLE BOB

Fill a tub (baby bath, bath tub, plastic wading pool) with water and float one apple per guest. Have the children kneel down and try to pick up an apple without using their hands. This can be done all at once or by turns. If you want to make it more challenging for older children, remove the stems.

VARIATIONS:
- Hang apples by a string (around the stem) from a tree.
- Hang doughnuts by a string from the ceiling and let the children eat them with their hands behind their heads (with or without blindfolds).

BALLOON BLOW

Blow up and tie one balloon for each child. Establish a race course with a starting and finish line (a dining room table is ideal). Have the children blow the balloons with their hands behind their backs. The first one to blow a balloon across the finish line is the winner. A ping-pong ball can be used in lieu of the balloon. If there are too many children to do this in one heat, divide them and have the winners race-off.

BALLOON HOP

Have the children race by hopping with a balloon between their knees.

BALLOON KICK

Have the children race by kicking a balloon to the finish line (again, no hands!).

BALLOON RELAY

Have as many balloons and chairs lined up as you have children. Place a blown balloon on the seat of each chair. From a starting line, have children race to a chair, sit down, pop the balloon and return back to the starting line. For a relay, use only one chair per team, but enough balloons for all the children.

BALLOON ROLL

Have the children race on their hands and knees, pushing a balloon with their noses (no hands!).

BALLOON STOMP

Fill a room or area with balloons. Let children sit, stomp, squeeze or do anything they want to in order to pop all the balloons.

BALLOON SURPRISE

Put a small object (raisin, bean, penny, candy, nut, marble, paper clip, bell, etc.) inside a balloon, then blow it up and tie it. Each child has to guess what is inside his balloon.

BALLOON TEAM RACE

Two children race holding one balloon between them without using their hands. Examples: at hips, ankles, back to back, heads, etc. First team to the finish line with an unpopped balloon is the winning team.

BEAN BAG TOSS
(see p. 121 for ways to make Bean Bags)

Go to an appliance store and ask for a big box (one that held a television set is a good size). Paint one side like a clown's face with an opening like a mouth for the target. Have children take turns trying to throw bean bags into the clown's mouth.

HAT OR BASKET TOSS: Place an upside-down hat or open basket at the far end of the room. Let the kids take turns throwing bean bags into the target.

RING THE BELL: Hang a cow bell by a string from a tree. Have the children stand behind a designated line and toss bean bags at the bell. The child who rings the bell the most times is the winner!

BICYCLE OBSTACLE COURSE

Using a long driveway, quiet street, nearby school grounds, track, etc., set up obstacles such as folding chairs, saw horses, garbage cans, buckets of water and so on. Assign an objective for each obstacle. (For example, ride twice around the saw horse, get off bicycle, crawl under saw horse, return to bicycle and proceed to next obstacle.) Then demonstrate the course for the participants. Have them go one at a time while the peanut gallery cheers from the sidelines. Be creative. Use "obstacles" you have around the house and garage. Also, make the course a challenge; the children will enjoy racing against a stop watch.

101

BRING THE PRINCESS (PRINCE) A GIFT

This is a guessing game for older children. There is a "trick" to it and the guests must try to figure it out. Go around the room and have each person mention a gift the princess or prince might like (a puppy, a necklace, some peaches, etc.). The chosen person (the guest of honor) accepts or rejects each gift. The trick is that the gift must start with the first letter of the royal person's name for her or him to like it. For example, Betsy likes blouses, boats, bananas, etc. Keep going until all the guests have figured it out.

BUTTON, BUTTON

Seat the children in a circle and choose one person to be It. Give that child a button. It holds the button between flat palms and stands in the middle of the circle. All the other children hold out their hands, palms together, and the person with the button passes his or her hands between everyone's in turn. The button will be dropped into one pair of hands, but It continues around the circle and then announces, "Button, button, who's got the button?" Everyone takes turns guessing. Whoever guesses correctly is the winner. Repeat the game until each child has been It.

CHAPEAU CHARADES

Have children grab a hat from a large box of hats and act out who would wear that particular one. For example: baker's hat, golf hat, cowboy hat, baseball cap.

CHEYENNE CHARADES

On slips of paper, write Indian-style names (i.e., White Dove, Running Water, Happy Bear). Place papers in a hat, basket or bowl. Have each child pick a slip of paper. Tell the children secretly what names they have chosen (as not all children can read at this age!). Each then will act out his or her name for the others to guess. This will become the child's name for the rest of the Pow-wow.

COPY CAT DANCE

Children stand in a circle. One child starts the dance with a certain gesture like stomping one foot. The group copies. The next child adds a gesture, like snapping two fingers together. The group now copies both gestures, and so on until each child has contributed a gesture to the dance. Play music that fits your party theme.

DROP THE CLOTHESPIN

Each child is given three clothespins (or toy farm animals, tokens, pennies, buttons, candies, etc.). Each then takes a turn kneeling over the back of a chair and attempting to drop the items into a milk bottle, mayonnaise jar, hat, basket or other container. The child with the greatest number of successes wins.

DUCK, DUCK, GOOSE (DROP THE HANDKERCHIEF)

Children sit in a circle. One child walks around the outside of the circle tapping each child on the head, saying "Duck." When the "tapping child" says "Goose" instead of "Duck", the Goose has to get up and chase the first child. The one who arrives at the empty space in the circle first sits down. The other child then becomes the "tapper."

Dropping a handkerchief (or feather, heart, star) in back of one player can replace the tapping.

EGG-IN-THE-SPOON RELAY

Divide the children into teams. Have each team line up one child behind the other. Give the first child in each line a soupspoon with an uncooked egg in it. Have the children with the eggs run to a designated point and back to the beginning of their line and pass the egg and spoon to the next person. The first team to complete the relay wins.

Be sure to have plenty of eggs on hand, and play this game outdoors!

EGG TOSS

This is usually pretty messy but always lots of fun. Do it outdoors or in a basement. Divide the children into teams of two. Give each team an egg. The object of the game is to toss the egg back and forth, then back up a few steps and toss again. The team that can stand the farthest apart (without breaking their egg, of course) is declared the winner. (Wipe up slippery broken egg at once. You *could* use hard-cooked eggs, but think what fun it is to have raw ones break—or be in danger of breaking!)

VARIATIONS: Water balloons, tomatoes.

104

FOLLOW THAT STRING

This game takes awhile to set up, but it's well worth the effort.

Buy a ball of string for each guest. Tie some sort of surprise to the end (a favor, cupcake, etc.) and hide it. Then unwind the ball of string, walking all over the yard or house . . . until the string is unwound or you decide it's long enough (not *too* long!). Then tie a bright-colored tag at the end with a guest's name on it.

At the party, the guests are each given a stick and must wind their strings around them, following the string until they find their surprises.

FOOTPRINT FOLLY

Trace your child's footprints on pieces of brightly colored construction paper. Have the child cut out about ten. Tape the footprints to the floor or sidewalk in such a way that they are difficult but not impossible to follow. Have the children take turns walking or running the course. You may wish to time them with a stop watch to establish a winner . . . or make a course for each guest. Have the children try the course backwards or barefoot and blindfolded.

GO FISH (GONE FISHIN')

Tack an old sheet or towel high enough to block the tallest child's view across a bedroom door. Make a fishing pole with a stick, a string and a clothespin. Have a helper (babysitter, older child or extra mom) stand behind the "water" and dispense prizes. Each child takes turns throwing his line in and waiting for a "bite" (helper tugs at the line). The child then pulls in his prize.

HAPPY BIRTHDAY (MARCO POLO)

This is a version of Blind Man's Bluff often played in a swimming pool. One person is blindfolded and counts to ten while the other people move about a designated playing area. The person then calls "freeze!" and everyone must stop where he or she is. The blindfolded It then tries to find and identify someone. In order to help himself or herself, It may say "Happy" and the other players must answer "Birthday!" (Or words that fit the party theme: "Pow" and "wow!"; "blast" and "off.") It may do this as often as necessary. The players may move their bodies in any manner to avoid It's touch, as long as one foot remains in place.

When someone is caught and identified, he or she becomes It.

HOT POTATO

Children sit in a circle and pass a potato around and around, without dropping it, while music plays. When the music stops, the person caught holding the potato is out.

VARIATIONS:
- Blast-off: moon rock (large rock)
- Pow-Wow: peace pipe (old pipe)
- Balloon: water balloon
- Pet Parade: stuffed animal
- Hearts Galore: Raggedy Ann doll
- Whodunnit: magnifying glass
- Hobo: knapsack
- Tea Party: tea cup or teaspoon

106

INDOOR/OUTDOOR DECATHLON

Choose any ten competitions from our suggestions or come up with some of your own. Keep cumulative scores and/or individual scores for medals and prizes, using the following:

5 points   1st place
4 points   2nd place
3 points   3rd place
2 points   4th place
1 point   5th place

1st, 2nd and 3rd places receive medals (see Favors for "Olympiad").

BACKWARDS RUN: Have children run backwards as fast as they can from the start to the finish line. (Hold this race on a relatively soft surface—grass, ground, carpeted floor!)

BASKETBALL: Child throws a ball of chosen size into cleaned trash can. Each child gets five turns. The child who gets it in the can the greatest number of times wins that individual event.

BEAN BAG TOSS: See Bean Bag ideas

BOOK-ON-THE-HEAD RACE: Child runs from starting point to finish line with a book on his or her head (no hands!). Eggs in a spoon can also be used if you are a brave soul or have the children outside, or use hard-cooked eggs.

BROAD JUMP (LONG JUMP):   Child runs to a certain marked area. When the child reaches the mark, he must jump forward as far as he can. Measure distances to determine winners.

FRISBEE THROW: Set up a target (i.e., a plate, etc.) in the middle of the yard and have each child attempt to throw the frisbee closest to the target in three tries. This game is like horseshoes with frisbees.

HOP-SKIP-JUMP: Similar to broad jump, except that after hitting the mark the child must hop (once), skip (once) and then jump. The child with the longest distance from the initial mark to the end of his jump wins.

HOPPING: Children simply hop from start to finish line as fast as they can. Jumping, skipping, crawling, etc. can all be substituted or added!

OBSTACLE COURSE: Same idea as bicycle obstacle course, only children run the course on foot. If it's a rainy day, go indoors and use furniture as the obstacles. This might create a bit more dust around, but who cares!

PILLOWCASE RACE: You'll need as many pillowcases as you have children. Have each child remove shoes, put both feet in a pillowcase and hop to the finish line while holding up the pillowcase.

SPRINTS: This is a full-out running race from one point to another. Use point scale as shown above.

I SEE SOMETHING

Children sit in a circle. One child spots an object in the room and says, "I see something *(blue)*." Each child in the circle takes a guess. If nobody guesses correctly, the child gives another clue, and so on. The child with the correct answer then gets to be the one giving clues.

I SPY THE LEPRECHAUN

This game is basically a backward version of Hide 'N Seek. It is best played outdoors. First, establish a home base such as a tree, garage door or stoop. Then the person who is picked to be "It" runs and hides from the others while they all cover their eyes at home base. In lieu of counting, the children sing the following chant to the tune of "Oh, My Darling Clementine":

"Are you ready? Are you ready? Are you ready
        Leprechaun?
Are you ready? Are you ready? Are you ready
        Leprechaun?"

If It yells back, "No!," then they keep singing until they get no response. When there is no answer, they know it is time to go find the leprechaun. When a child spies the leprechaun he must run back and touch base before the leprechaun catches him. The object is for the leprechaun to catch one of the children, who is then It for the next round.

_____MAY I? (MOTHER MAY I?)

All the players line up facing "Mother" (one of the children), who is standing ten to fifteen feet away. The object of the game is to be the first person to reach "Mother" and take over for the next game.

"Mother" addresses each child in turn and says, "_____, you may take two baby steps." That person must ask "Mother, may I?" and Mother grants permission with "Yes, you may." The person is then allowed to take the two steps. If someone fails to ask "Mother, may I?", he or she must go back to the starting line.

"Mother" may use her discretion as to how many

steps each person may take and what kind (baby, giant, backwards, hopping, scissors, waddling, etc.).

Another aspect of the game is cheating! The players may try to sneak steps while "Mother" isn't watching. If she catches them, they must go back to the start.

VARIATIONS: "Raggedy Ann, may I?","Hobo, may I?", "Easter Bunny, may I?", etc.

MEMORY GAME

Put an assortment of household items on a tray. Bring it into the party room, pass it around, then take it away. Pass out slips of paper and pencils. Ask the children to list as many objects as they can remember. The person with the longest correct list wins.

This can be a team competition. Put the teams in two different rooms and show them identical trays.

Young children can draw pictures or dictate their answers.

MUSICAL HEARTS

Tape big red or pink construction paper hearts to the floor, making sure that you have one less heart than you do children. Play music while children dance around. When you stop the music, each child must run and stand on a heart. The child without a heart to stand on must stay out, but gets to operate the record player for the next round. Before starting the music again, remove one heart. Repeat this until only one child remains.

NONCOMPETITIVE VERSION: Instead of removing a child, have children share positions on hearts until all the children are on one heart.

Musical footprints, pillows or chairs can replace hearts. For other parties use shamrocks, stars, egg shapes, pumpkins, etc. For a sit-down version, see Hot Potato.

MYSTERY EGG

Inside plastic eggs (available at grocery stores and dime stores at Easter time) place a piece of hard candy, a penny, a walnut, a peanut, a small amount of water, a small amount of sand or a gum ball. Make each egg's contents different. Have the children pick up each egg and guess what is inside.

MYSTERY PERSON

Blindfold all the children and tap one of them on the head to designate the mystery person. Then instruct the children to move about and ask each other, "Are you the mystery person?" No one is to answer the question except the mystery person, who does so by squeezing that person's hand. Now there are two mystery persons and they continue holding hands until eventually all the children are holding hands and the game is over.

VARIATIONS:
- Blast-off: "Are you the astronaut?"
- Bike Road-Day-O: "Are you the policeman?"
- Olympiad: "Are you the gold medalist?"
- Hobo: "Are you the hobo?"
- Tea Party: "Are you the princess?"
- Whodunnit: "Are you the detective?"

111

PASS THE APPLE

Group children into two teams and line them up. One child from each team places an apple (or orange) under his chin. This child must pass the apple to the next teammate, via the chin, without the use of hands. First team to finish wins. You may also pass eggs from spoon to spoon (or ping-pong balls, walnuts, etc.). The children can either hand-carry the spoons or hold them between their teeth!

PENNY HUNT

Go to your bank and get a roll or two of shiny pennies; then hide them (inside or outside). Give each child a cup, can or bag and let them hunt. Variation: nuts (in the shell), penny candy, marbles, etc.

(We once hid peanuts all around the yard the night before a party. The next day, no nuts to find! The squirrels got there first!)

PENNY PITCH

Place a hat upside down at the end of the room. Give each child ten pennies (get a roll of shiny new ones from your bank). Have the children stand back and take turns pitching pennies into the hat. The child who gets the most in the hat is the winner.

Repeat as often as children wish. Let them take their pennies home.

VARIATION: Throw nuts, playing cards or candy into a basket, bowl or box.

112

PIN THE . . . (NOSE ON THE CLOWN, FEATHER ON THE INDIAN, KNAPSACK ON THE HOBO, TAIL ON THE EASTER BUNNY, ETC.)

A variation on the classic Pin-the-Tail-on-the-Donkey.

Paint a target on a sheet or large piece of butcher paper and attach to the wall with masking tape or thumbtacks. Design the target to comply with the theme of the party. Prepare as many pin-ons (noses, knapsacks or whatever) as you have guests. This can be done with construction paper and rolled masking tape to secure to the target.

The child is blindfolded, spun around and pointed in the proper direction. The child who comes closest to the "bull's eye" is declared the winner.

RAIN DANCE

Find some American Indian music at the library. Play music while children, in their costumes, swing toma-hawk shakers and dance. When you stop the music, the dancers must hold their positions until you start the music again. Any child who moves while the music is not playing must sit down.

RED LIGHT, GREEN LIGHT

At one end of a driveway or quiet street, have children line up on bicycles. At the other end have one person (Mom, Dad or helper) call the signals. "Green light" means that children ride as quickly and as far as possible until signal caller calls "red light," which means they all must stop. Anyone not stopping is out. The first child to

113

reach the finish line is the winner. This, of course, can be played on foot.

SANDBOX SEARCH

If you have a backyard sandbox, buy a bag of plastic animals, soldiers, play jewelry, etc. and hide them in the sandbox.

SCAVENGER HUNT

Divide the children into pairs. Give each team a bag and a different list of ten items. The children then go from house to house in your neighborhood (explain the boundaries *carefully*), asking for items. Set a time limit (thirty minutes) and honk your car horn or ring a bell to signal the finish. The team that gathers the most listed items wins. It's wise to call your neighbors and warn them!

Suggested Items: Hair curler, used light bulb, red button, picture of a TV star, three rubber bands, an old comb, paper plate, safety pin, walnut, popcorn kernel, toilet paper tube, cupcake paper, yellow pencil, coffee can, piece of bread, empty matchbook, bottle cap, toothpick, old lipstick, brown shoelace. Have your own child use his or her imagination to help you make up the other children's lists.

SECRET WORD STORY TIME

Choose a short story before the party begins. Notice which words appear with frequency. Choose as many words as you will have children. Be sure they are words that can be acted out.

114

Confidentially assign a different word to each child. When the child hears his or her word in the story, it's the cue to stand up and act it out. For example, "cow" might be expressed by holding hands up like horns and saying "moo!"

SHOE RACE

All the children remove their shoes and deposit them in a laundry basket or box. Place the box at the far end of the room. At the command, children race to the box, find their own shoes, put them on and race back to the starting line.

A variation is to fill the basket with Mom's and Dad's shoes. Have the children find a matching pair, put them on and return to the starting line.

This game can also be played with mittens, gloves, hats or entire suits of clothing (Daddy's pants, shirts, shoes, socks; Mother's dress, shoes, hat, etc.).

SIMON SAYS (BIRDS FLY)

Children line up. One child is "Simon" and faces the group. Simon gives the children a series of commands, preceding each command with "Simon says." The children do as "Simon says" (Simon says, "Touch your nose") unless Simon fails to say "Simon says." Anyone who follows a command not preceded by "Simon says" is out. The last person left standing is declared the winner. Call the game "Christopher Says" (using the birthday child's name).

115

VARIATION:
A simplified version for younger children is called "Birds Fly." All the children squat, and each time the leader (you) says "Birds fly," they all stand up and flap their wings. However, if the leader says "Elephants fly" (or uses any other animal), they remain squatting. Any child who stands then is out.

SPACE FLIGHT

Paint a grocery box (tuck flaps inside so it is open) bright yellow or silver, or cover it with bright contact paper. Punch a hole in each of the four sides and tie on a piece of string. Bring the four strings together in the middle and tie. Add one long piece of string and suspend the box from the ceiling with a strong thumbtack, to hang about a foot above children's heads. Give each child an 8½" x 11" piece of paper and show how to make a paper airplane. Daddy may need to lend his expertise.

The children take turns trying to throw their planes into the box.

SPELLING SCRAMBLE

From 8½" × 11" paper, cut shapes that fit your party theme (hearts, eggs, stars) for each guest. Punch two holes at the top of each and thread with enough yarn to enable them to hang around the child's neck. Write one letter on each piece of paper in order to spell out a special message (I L-O-V-E Y-O-U, H-A-P-P-Y 7, L-A-U-R-E-N). Hang a letter on each child and see how quickly they can line up in order. Then exchange letters and do it again. Older children may be able to come up with new words of their own.

116

SPONGE BOWLING

Set up sponges in a pyramid shape. Let children take turns at knocking them down, either by rolling a tennis ball or tossing a bean bag.

TELEPHONE

All the children sit in a circle. One person thinks of a special message and whispers it to his neighbor. He, in turn, whispers it to the next person and so on around the circle until the message returns to the person who sent it. Then that person announces the message he has received as well as the original. It's amazing how different the two can be.

For very little children, the message can be initiated by the adult, and be short: "Burger and fries" or "Hug an elephant" or something else somewhat, but not too, familiar.

TREASURE HUNT

Make up a series of clues and write them on slips of paper. Hide the clues around the house. Direct the children to each clue in order. For example:

Clue #1: "Sugar and spice and everything nice; where is the clue, you'd better think twice" (clue in spice rack).

Clue #2: "Ring-ring, who's there; you'll find a clue I know not where" (under the telephone).

Clue #3: "Round and round and round she goes; it plays songs everyone knows" (stereo).

Clue #4: "Watch this box and you will see, your favorite program, 1-2-3" (television).

117

Clue #5: "I'm so tired I could weep; where, oh, where can I go to sleep" (bed).

Clue #6: "There's a word that I can't spell. Oh, I know this book will tell" (dictionary).

Clue #7: "Socks and pants and shorts and shirt; boy, my clothes are full of dirt" (washer).

Clue #8: "Knock, knock, please be neat; just remember—wipe your feet" (door mat).

Clue #9: "Tick-tock, tick-tock; is it time to take a walk?" (clock).

Clue #10: "Br-r-r I'm cold from head to feet; and, boy, I've got good things to eat" (refrigerator).

Read the first clue aloud to the group and let them all hunt together, or make up two sets of clues and divide into teams.

Have the last clue be the refrigerator or freezer and the "treasure" will be your dessert or cake.

TWISTER

On the back patio or walk chalk numbers 1 through 10, jumbled up and out of sequence. Or you may tape the numbers, boldly written on construction paper, to the floor indoors. Write each number (except 1) again on a slip of paper and place them in a basket. Each child takes a turn, starting with the left foot on number 1. You then draw a number from the basket to decide where he or she should put the right foot, left hand, left foot, etc. The fun is in seeing how tangled up a child can get.

WATCH WHERE YOU SIT

Arrange chairs in a circle, facing in. Cut out paper shapes of hearts, shamrocks, eggs, balloons or pumpkins and write a silly activity on each one. For example, write: "Stand on your head," "Tell everyone who your favorite friend is" or "Hop five times." Gear the activities to the age level. Draw pictures if necessary for pre-schoolers.

Tape the shapes to the underside of each chair. Pick someone to be It and blindfold him or her. Ask the other children to march around the chairs until It yells, "Stop!" When they all have found a chair, It points to someone who must look under his or her chair and perform the activity indicated. That person then becomes It.

WHAT AM I? (ANIMAL CHARADES)

A child pulls a picture of an animal out of a hat or basket. He or she then has to act out the animal while the other children guess what it is. The first child to guess correctly then gets the next turn.

WHO AM I?

Think up characters that fit the party theme ahead of time, and prepare one for each child. If the children are able to read, you may simply write each character on a piece of paper.* If not, then cut out a picture of the subject from a magazine or draw one. To play the game, pin a paper on each child's back without showing it to him or her. The child then asks "yes-no" questions of members of the group in turn in order to guess "Who Am I?"

SUGGESTIONS:
• "Blast-off"—fictional space characters, astronauts

---

*For a Valentine's Day party, draw the subject on red paper hearts; for a Hallowe'en Party, use orange paper pumpkins; for St. Patrick's Day, green paper shamrocks . . . etc.

- "Pow-wow"—famous Native americans (Pocahontas, Geronimo)
- "Whodunnit"—famous detectives (Columbo, Sherlock Holmes, Dick Tracy)
- Television characters
- Movie stars
- Athletes

WINK, WINK

This is a nice, quiet game involving lots of eye contact, and can be played again and again. Seat the children in a large circle and pass out folded slips of paper. All slips of paper have an "O", except for one which has an "X". That person with the "X" is It and must eliminate the others one by one. He does so by catching someone's eye and winking. That person waits a second (in order to avoid giving it away) and announces, "I'm out."

People may at any time guess who is doing the winking. If the guess is correct the game is over and it's time for another round. If the guess is incorrect, however, the "guessee" and the "guessor" are out.

If the winner is clever enough to eliminate everyone without being caught, he deserves a prize!

18

Activities

BACKYARD MURAL

Call the printing department at your local newspaper and ask them for their left over "end rolls" of newsprint. They usually give it away free!

Tack the newsprint all along your back fence, garage door or other appropriate location. Prepare different colors of poster paint in cleaned soup cans and provide a long, thick brush for each. Be sure to tell the children to keep the blue brush in the blue paint, the red brush in the red paint and so on.

If this is incorporated in a warm-weather party, ask the guests to wear bathing suits. When the mural is complete, turn on the hose and let the children wash each other off!

BEAN BAGS

Bean bags are a very versatile toy that can be used in games played by all ages. Needless to say, bean bags don't have to be filled with beans! You can substitute unpopped popcorn, peas, rice, or anything that you have in your kitchen cupboards.

If you have a sewing machine (or easy access to one), you can grab some scraps of material and sew a bag simply by sewing three sides (right sides together). Turn right sides out, fill with "beans," sew up the fourth side, pink the edge and there you have it!

A sturdy sandwich-size plastic bag, half filled, with a rubber band to secure the top, makes a surprisingly long-lasting bag. Make sure that you wrap the rubber band *many* times around to insure that you won't have beans everywhere. Also keep an eye out to be sure some quiet four-year-old doesn't slip behind a chair, patiently remove the rubber band and play "Here Comes the Bride," or try to eat the filling.

Bean bags can double as take-home favors.

BEAN BAG ACTIVITY

BLEACH BOTTLE SCOOPS: All this takes is a little forethought. Save two or more 2-quart plastic bleach bottles—rinsed thoroughly—cut as shown. The kids will love tossing a bean bag back and forth with them.

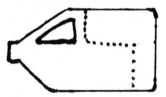

BEAN BAG TARGET

A sturdy cardboard box, decorated and with a hole cut out of the center, will work well. Place the target against a wall so it doesn't tumble over.

Another approach is to cut a large square box in half on the diagonal so as to make a tent shape when placed on the floor. Then cut a hole on one side for the target.

COOKING ACTIVITIES

Boys and girls *both* get enthusiastic over "trying their hand" in the kitchen. Here are some ideas that are sure hits.

PRETZELS
(4 children/batch)

4 T. warm water
½ t. sugar
½ t. dry yeast
½ cup flour
pinch salt

Combine all the ingredients. Knead the dough for five minutes (all the children can take turns at this). Cut the dough into four pieces. Roll each piece into a long rope. Loop in pretzel shape. Brush with a beaten egg.*
Bake at 425°F. for fifteen minutes. Cool.

CREATIVE COOKIES AND CUPCAKES Using your favorite sugar cookie recipe, our recipe, or "slice-and-bake" refrigerator dough, make a large batch of cookies ahead of time. You can freeze them and then thaw on party day.

Supply the children with tube frostings, candies, carob chips, nuts and raisins for decorating and turn them loose.

Instead of cookies, you can make cupcakes, freezing them and defrosting on the day of the party. Use the

*Option: sprinkle with Kosher salt.

123

same supplies for decorating, and also add a big bowl or two of frosting, flavored and/or colored.

COOKIE RECIPE
½ cup margarine
½ cup sugar
½ cup dark molasses
¼ cup water
2½ cups flour
¾ t. salt
½ t. soda
¾ t. ginger
⅛ t. nutmeg
⅛ t. allspice

Cream sugar and margarine. Add remaining ingredients, cover and chill two to three hours. Roll dough on floured board ¼" thick, cut with cookie cutter and place on ungreased cookie sheet. Bake ten to twelve minutes at 375°F.

FINGER LICKIN' FINGER PAINTIN'

Here are some ideas for finger "painting" materials that are fun, if messy. They can be done on paper (it's best to wet it first) directly on a washable table top, or on a paper plate so they can eat the finished product. If it's a nice day you may even let the kids "paint" on the sidewalk or patio, followed by a "hose-off."

Pudding
Whipped cream
Mashed potatoes (whip with electric mixer
  and milk)
Cream of Wheat
Gelatin (semisoft)

You may wish to add food color, drop by drop, as the

124

children are painting. They will enjoy seeing the color blend in, as well as learning how colors are made (i.e., red + blue = purple, yellow + blue = green, etc.).

Another similar activity is to put soft gelatin or thick poster paint in a zip-lock bag (or a plastic bag tied tightly with a rubber band). Make one for each child (approximately ½ cup in each bag). Make different colors and let the children trade. They will enjoy making various designs with their fingers, then shaking the bag and starting over.

FRUIT FACE

Give each guest a potato, apple or orange and a handful of wooden toothpicks. Then present a bowl full of raisins, marshmallows, carrot slices, grapes, rinsed fruit cocktail, banana slices, etc., plus parsley, mustard greens, carrot tops, etc. for hair.

Give a prize for the prettiest, ugliest, funniest, etc., making sure each guest wins one.

HOMEMADE GREASE PAINT

BASIC RECIPE
2 T. white shortening
5 t. cornstarch
1 t. white flour

Blend with a flat spoon. Makes enough for one or two faces.

Brown: add powdered cocoa
Other colors: add food coloring

125

PEACE PIPE BUBBLES

1 part dishwashing liquid
1 part water

Mix together and place in individual containers for each child. For the Hobo party, but inexpensive corncob pipes at a variety store and put the soap mixture in tin cans. For the Indian party, buy a package of bubble pipes and put the soap in small paper cups.

PIÑATA

This wonderful Mexican fiesta custom can be adapted for any of the theme parties. It is basically a papier-mâché ball filled with candy and toys, suspended by heavy string from a broomstick. Hold the piñata up and let the children take turns trying to break it with a stick. To make it more of a challenge for older children, blindfold them and twirl them around.

Making the piñata is pretty messy, but tackle it with your child and you'll both have fun. It's really very easy, and you probably have all the materials around the house. You will need:

a large balloon
flour and water (mix it in a pie tin)
newspaper torn in strips
poster paint

Cover a working surface with newspaper. Blow up the balloon and balance it in a box or pan. Saturate each strip of paper with paste and smooth it over the balloon. Cover the whole balloon in this fashion and let it dry. Be sure to leave a small opening at the top. (You may have to let one side dry before you can cover the other side. It takes a day or so to dry, depending on your climate, so start this project well before your party.)

126

After the piñata is dry, pop the balloon and remove it. Then paint and decorate the piñata according to your theme:

CLOWNS—Clown face with crepe paper hair and party hat

POW-WOW—Indian face with a feather and headband

HEARTS GALORE—Raggedy Ann's face with yarn hair

PET PARADE—Cat face with construction paper ears and pipe-cleaner whiskers

HALLOWE'EN—Jack-O-lantern or witch

CHRISTMAS—Santa or snowman
When the paint is dry, fill your masterpiece with small toys, goodies and confetti. Don't make it too heavy or it will break too soon. Tie a knot in the end of a piece of heavy cord (clothes line is great) and put the free end into the opening and then out through a small slit at the tip of the piñata. For added security, tape the slit. Tie the other end of the string to a broom handle. The person who holds the piñata can be as playful as he pleases, depending on how long you want the activity to last!

PRINTING

Printing is another enjoyable and quiet activity. Children love to make monograms or just designs from materials they never dreamed of using. Again, the plastic dropcloth or tablecloth is an essential! We suggest using poster paints as the colors are bright, can be mixed for varied tones and are water soluble for easy clean up! Place different colors and combinations in a couple of muffin tins, set out assorted "stamps" and paper, and let the children go wild creating.

STAMP SUGGESTIONS:

> Thick potato, carrot or turnip slices (Mom or Dad can carve out a raised design or initials)
> Apple, orange, lemon slices
> Sponges, corks, toothbrushes, combs, cookie cutters, potato masher
> Erasers carved with a raised design
> Clay carved with a raised design

Let the children experiment, giving as little direction as possible. Younger children can print with the materials; older ones may want to carve their own stamps, using table knives.

PUPPETS

Children always enjoy making and playing with puppets. You may wish to make this a central theme of your party or just an added activity.

FINGER PUPPETS: Give each child a 2" × 3" piece of heavy paper and finepoint felt pens. Tell the children to lay their index fingers on the paper and draw two dots at the top and two at the bottom to measure the width. Then draw a face between the dots. When finished, roll the paper around a finger and secure with masking tape.

GLOVE: Cut the fingers off an old pair of white gloves (try the Salvation Army if you don't have any). Give each child a glove finger, a needle and thread or glue and a pen or pencil. Fill a muffin tin with buttons, sequins, lace, rick rack, yarn, felt scraps, etc. and let the children create!

128

PEN: Buy a selection of colored ball point or fine point felt-tip pens. Let the children draw faces, hair, hats, bow ties, etc. on the inside of their index fingers or thumbs.

SOCK: Finally a use for all those socks without mates at the bottom of your drawer! Give each child an old sock, needle and thread or white glue, plus a big selection of fabric scraps, trim, buttons, ribbon, etc. Give the children puppet suggestions that tie in with the theme of the party; i.e., pets, animals, clowns.

PAPER BAG: A folded lunch-size bag makes a great puppet. All you need is a bag for each child, crayons, glue, scissors (optional), colored paper scraps, yarn, etc. This can double for a take-home bag when the party is over.

FIST-FACE: Simply tuck your thumb inside your fist and draw a face on the side of your fist with a ball point pen. Be sure the upper lip is on your index finger and the lower lip is on your thumb. Now wiggle your thumb slightly to make your puppet talk.

PENCIL AND TACK: Give each child a small piece of heavy paper (shirt cardboard is good), colored pens, a pencil and a tack. Have them color a face or whole body, cut it out and tack it to the eraser on the pencil.

When the puppets are completed, the children will want to put on a show. So have a "stage" ready. Here are some ideas:

Pull the sofa out from the wall and let the puppeteer crouch down behind it.

Clothespin a tablecloth or sheet between two chairs.

Turn a card table on its side.

Open a low window and have the puppeteer stand outside.

Tape the lid of a large dress box to the top of a table.

If you're feeling energetic, get an appliance box, cut a hole in one side and paint the outside.

ROCK ART

Have the children gather smooth rocks and wash them. Then provide paints, brushes, bits of paper, felt scraps and individual glue containers (cut-up egg cartons work beautifully). Let them create animals, monsters, dolls or just pretty rocks. It is also fun to decorate walnuts, whole or half shell.

SCULPTURE

A quiet, creative activity for children of all ages is molding clay or dough. You'll need a work area for the children. This area can be inside or outside, on the floor, on the ground or at a table. A plastic dropcloth or inexpensive plastic tablecloth is great to use, because the clay doesn't stick to it and it is easy to clean up. The clay or dough is inexpensive and simple to make with ingredients from your kitchen. Here are a few recipes from which to choose:

INEDIBLE DOUGH
½ cup water
1 cup flour
⅔ cup salt
2 T. oil
1 T. alum (found at drugstore)
food coloring

Mix all ingredients except water. Color the water and slowly add to other ingredients until the mixture arrives at a consistency like bread dough. Each batch of clay can have a different color. Clay may be stored in plastic bags in the refrigerator for a long time!

EDIBLE DOUGH

Mix together: 1 (18 oz.) jar of peanut butter
6½ T. honey
Add slowly: Dry milk and flour until you
arrive at desired texture.

The children can shape this dough, decorate it with coconut, raisins, M & Ms, etc., and eat it. You might want to put each child's sculpture in a plastic bag and refrigerate it until it's time to go home and give as a take-home favor.

BAKED DOUGH

This is another way of making a favor that's fun. After the children have designed their creations, you bake them. The next day your birthday child can deliver the finished product with his or her thank-you note.

Recipe: 1 cup salt
2 cups flour
⅔ cup water (more or less)
2 T. vegetable oil

Bake at 250°F. for several hours.

If you are pressed for time, store-bought Silly Putty or clay can be obtained from your local variety store.

TRANSFERS

CONTACT PAPER TRANSFERS: Buy some clear contact paper (available by the yard at hardware or paint stores). Give each child a piece, along with some scissors and a magazine. Peel the backing and stick contact paper to a selected picture. Smooth it and then cut it out of the magazine. Put the picture between two pieces of brown paper bag and iron lightly with a warm iron. Then submerge the picture in water and gently rub the magazine paper off. *Voilà!* The picture stays on the contact paper!

This can now be put on a smooth piece of wood, glass or cardboard.

Recipes

(Recipes are listed in alphabetical order within each category, as shown below)

BEVERAGES

Juice Brenner
Mmmm Good
Mocha Flip
Moonshine
O. J. "Sip"-Son
Orange-up
Puppy Punch

Puzzle Punch
Razzamatazz
Shirley's Twist
Sweet Tea
Tropical Punch
Yogurt Shake

ENTREES

Beans 'n Weiners
Chain-o-Lunch
Cheese/Bacon Dogs
Chili Corn Cups

Corn Bread
Corn Dog Squares
Crepes for Kids
Grilled Cheese Loverlies

Meat Loafers
Moonwich
Pancake Rolls
Pigs-in-a-Blanket
Pizza Wheels
Pow-wow Pups
Pretty as a Princess Puffs
　(with Easy Cream Puff
　Recipe)
Quick Chili
Ragamuffins

Sandwiches
　Grease Paint Sandwiches
　Guess What? Sandwiches
　PB & ? Sandies
　Pumpkin Sand-Witches
　Teatime Sandwiches
Sloppy Joes
Tacos
Terrific Turnovers
Tuna Burgers/Tuna Boats
Tuna Salad
Witches' Brew

GOOD-FOR-YA'S

Animal Salad
Angeled Eggs
Antipasto
Apple Rings
Banana Ships
Garbage Can Lids
Roasted Pumpkin Seeds

Safari Salad
Stuffed Celery
Sunshine Salad
Tepee Treats
Trail Mix
Tropical Fruit
What's Next Salad

TRICKY TREATS

Chocolate Toasties
Finger Gelatin Dessert
Fudgies
Gelatin Eggs

Popcorn Balls
Snow Cones
Special Cupcakes
Yipes Stripes Gelatin

STUFF-ON-A-STICK

Freezer Pops
Frozen Banana
Fruit-tail Pops

Lollipops
Popcorn-pops

134

ICE CREAM DESSERTS

Clown Cones
Flowerpot Ice Cream
Homemade Ice Cream Bars
Ice Cream or Yogurt Balls
Ice Cream Sandies
Individual Ice Cream Pies

Make-a-Sundae
Perfect Parfaits
Raggedy Ann Cones
Snowballs
Toddler Ice Cream
Yogurt Pops

CAKES AND COOKIES

American Flag Cake
Animal Crackers
Applesauce Cake
Boxcar Cake
Carousel Cake
Carrot Cake
Carrot Cookies
Clown Cake
Clue Cookies
Cupcake Baskets
Detective's ID Cake
Doll Carriage Cake

Gingerbread Cake
Heart Cake
Jack-o-Lantern Cake
Nut Torte
Olympiad Cake
Petit Fours
Rocket Cake
Stop Sign Cake
Sugar Cookies
Tin Can Cupcakes
Totem Pole Cake

BEVERAGES

There are a variety of disposable cups on the market. Paper and styrofoam are inexpensive and come in several sizes. Thin plastic cups are a little more durable. Hard plastic ones are more expensive but can be decorated with the child's name and thus double as a place-card or favor.

Most children like ice cubes in their drinks. Try putting a piece of fruit or a mint leaf in each cube before

135

freezing, or make the ice cubes with diluted fruit juice instead of water. Don't make miniature cubes, as they are too easily swallowed.

JUICE BRENNER
Mix 1 (6 oz.) can frozen grape juice concentrate and 1½ cups milk in a blender.

Mmmm GOOD
In a blender, mix a cup of fresh or frozen strawberries, 2 T. honey and 4 cups milk. Blend until smooth.

MOCHA FLIP

Dissolve: ⅓ cup instant cocoa
1 T. instant decaffeinated coffee
¼ cup sugar

In   ¼ cup hot water

Add   1 qt. cold milk

Blend.

MOONSHINE
Place a big scoop of lemon sherbet in a tall glass of 7-Up.

O.J. "SIP"-SON
Combine 1 cup milk, 2 cups orange juice and 1 T. powdered sugar in a blender. Serves 8 children.
Variations: Add a raw egg, ripe banana, vanilla ice cream, or 7-Up.

ORANGE-UP
Mix 1 part orange juice to 3 parts 7-Up. Garnish with an orange slice.
Variation: Add a scoop of vanilla ice cream or orange sherbet.

136

PUPPY PUNCH
Mix tropical punch with orange juice. Serve with ice and decorative straw.

PUZZLE PUNCH
Add a few drops of food coloring to a glass of apple juice. Make each glass a different color.

RAZZAMATAZZ
Mix 1 part cranberry juice, or any red fruit juice, with 2 parts ginger ale or 7-Up. Garnish with a scoop of vanilla ice cream and a colorful straw. Serve in a tall glass.

SHIRLEY'S TWIST
Mix ginger ale and grenadine in tall or stemmed glass. Add a fresh fruit garnish on the rim of the glass.
Garnish suggestions: strawberry, lemon, lime, pineapple, orange.

SWEET TEA
Brew a pot of very light herb tea and flavor with a powdered orange juice drink and honey. Serve warm in fancy tea cups.

TROPICAL PUNCH
Garnish a glass of lemonade with a bamboo skewer of tropical fruit: pineapple chunks, banana slices or orange sections.

YOGURT SHAKE
Blend:
¾ cup of pineapple, orange, cranberry
  or apple juice
1 cup plain yogurt
1 ripe banana
2½ T. honey

Serve in small glasses and garnish with a dollop of whipped cream, fresh fruit, etc.

ENTREES

BEANS 'N WEINERS
Heat canned pork 'n beans. Add slices of broiled hot dogs. Serve in small cups.

CHAIN-O-LUNCH
String any of the following together with a needle and thread:

strawberries, grapes, apple chunks
banana slice, pear, raisin
carrot slices, celery, zucchini, beans
cheese cubes
lunch meat strips/hot dog slices

Be sure to tell the children not to eat the thread. Skewers can be substituted, but we wouldn't trust too many children with a skewer!

CHEESE/BACON DOGS
Butterfly frankfurters and fill with grated cheddar cheese. Wrap a strip of bacon around the frankfurter. Secure with toothpicks. You may either broil or bake until cheese melts and franks begin to brown. Serve warm. You may wish to place each cheese/bacon dog in a hot dog bun, cut in half, and serve half per child, as these are rich.

CHILI CORN CUPS
Make your favorite chili with beans recipe or try the easy method on page 143. While the chili simmers, prepare corn bread batter (from a packaged mix or recipe on page 139) and pour into tinfoil cupcake cups,

one tablespoon per cup. Bake at 400°F. for 10 minutes. Remove. Fill the rest of the cup with chili, top with grated cheddar, a teaspoon of sour cream or cottage cheese.

CORN BREAD

1 cup corn meal
1 cup flour
4 T. sugar
1 T. baking powder
dash salt
6 T. shortening
1 cup milk
1 egg

Mix first 5 ingredients—add shortening, stir with fork until crumbly. Add egg and milk. Mix well. Bake in an 8" x 8" greased pan in a hot (425°F.) oven for 25 minutes or until done.

CORN DOG SQUARES
If you are looking for an easy yet different entrée for children, this is a goodie. Simply mix a 14-oz. package of corn bread mix according to package directions or use the recipe above and pour into a greased jelly roll pan. Sprinkle with ½ cup grated cheddar cheese and 5 cooked frankfurters sliced into 9 slices each. Bake in a 400°F. oven until golden brown. Cut into squares. Serve warm.

CRÊPES FOR KIDS
The mystique of crêpes has been pierced! They can be easier to make than pancakes!
2 eggs
⅔ cup milk
⅓ cup water
¾ cup flour

1 t. double-acting baking powder
2 T. powdered sugar

While blending the eggs, milk and water in your uncovered electric blender, sift the remaining ingredients into the blender. *Voilà!*

Rub a small amount of oil in a small iron skillet or crêpe pan. Save the oily paper towel and wipe the pan between the cooking of each crêpe. Heat the pan over medium high heat. When the pan is very hot, remove it from the heat and pour about 2 tablespoons of batter into the pan. Gently swirl the pan to distribute the batter evenly over the bottom in a thin film. Place on the heat for about 60 seconds. Turn over and cook for about another 30 seconds.

Flip the crêpe out of the pan, add filling and serve or place on a paper towel. Always put the filling on the second side as it is not as smooth as the first side. Traditionally, the French always throw away the first crêpe. But our recipe is so terrific you won't have the heart!

Repeat the above procedure and alternate the crêpes with wax paper. Put them in a plastic bag or a pie tin. They can be stored in the refrigerator or frozen.

When you are ready to serve the crêpes, fill them with honey, jelly, jam, butter/cinnamon/powdered sugar, fresh fruit, whipped cream and fruit or your own concoction. Roll and serve.

For cheese crêpes, sprinkle grated cheddar, jack or Swiss cheese to cover the crepe sparsely while it is cooking on the first side. Cook until cheese melts. Remove from the heat, fold in half and then half again and remove from the pan onto the child's plate. The children won't mind the assembly line serving, as watching the procedure is very entertaining!

GRILLED CHEESE LOVERLIES
Slice cheese and place on a piece of sliced bread. Using heart, shamrock, animal or Christmas cookie

cutters, cut out sandwiches. Broil open faced until cheese melts. Serve warm.

MEAT LOAFERS
Mix the following:

1 lb. lean ground beef
¾ can cream of mushroom soup
1 cup bread crumbs
⅓ cup fresh parsley (cut with scissors)
dash salt
dash garlic salt (optional for some kids)
small can chopped olives

Grease a muffin tin and pour ½ t. catsup in each before filling with mixture (or mold in foil cupcake cups). Bake 40 minutes at 350°F.

MOONWICH
Split bagels, then cut in half (thus, crescent shaped). Top with grated cheddar cheese and broil, or top with tuna, egg salad, ham or chicken spread.

PANCAKE ROLLS
Prepare your favorite pancake recipe, making each pancake about 4″ in diameter. Layer cooked pancakes with pieces of waxed paper, cover and refrigerate. Just before serving, place a dollop of whipped cream and a piece of fruit on each pancake. Roll the pancake and secure with a toothpick. Fruit suggestions are a strawberry, apple slice, peach slice or banana slice. Canned fruit pie filling makes a delicious, though not as nutritious, substitute filling.

For the blueberry pancakes found in the All-American Jamboree, you can use a blueberry batter recipe and fill with blueberries or any other "patriotic" combination you wish to choose.

You may wish to warm the pancakes before serving, but, believe it or not, they are just as good cold!

PIGS-IN-A-BLANKET
Young children are small eaters, so one of these should suffice. Gear the number of "pigs" you make to the number of guests. We have found that sausage (link style) is a big hit. You may also use weiners, vienna sausage or a facsimile thereof. Cook the sausage and drain. Using refrigerator canned biscuits, flatten a biscuit on a floured board and wrap it around a sausage and place on a greased cookie sheet. Bake slightly longer than biscuit directions. "Pigs" may be accompanied by mustard or catsup for dipping.

PIZZA WHEELS
Spread split English muffin with marinara sauce and top with any of the following:

salami
pepperoni
olives
mushrooms
onions
green peppers
cooked hamburger
cooked sausage

Cover with grated cheese (mozzarella, cheddar, and Swiss or jack—a mixture is delicious). Place on cookie sheet and bake in a preheated 450°F. oven a few minutes, until cheese bubbles.

POW-WOW PUPS
Slice broiled or boiled franks crosswise and top with a small hunk of cheddar cheese. Spear with a toothpick. Allow 3 or 4 per child (try chicken or turkey franks).

142

PRETTY AS A PRINCESS PUFFS
Stuff cream puffs (see recipe below) with tuna, egg salad, or your favorite filling.

EASY CREAM PUFFS
In a saucepan combine ½ cup water with 4 T. of butter. Bring mixture to the bubbling stage over medium heat. Add ½ cup of flour, all at once. Turn off the heat but keep beating the mixture over the hot burner until it becomes a shiny ball and doesn't stick to the sides of the pan. Remove from heat. Add 2 eggs (one at a time), beating 30 seconds between each addition. Spoon onto greased cookie sheet. Bake at 425°F. for 10 minutes, turn heat down to 350° for 25 minutes longer. Cool, split and fill. Yield: approximately 20.

QUICK CHILI
Brown 1 lb. of hamburger. Drain. Add a #2 can of chili beans, dash of chili powder and salt to taste. Simmer.

RAGAMUFFINS
Spread softened cream cheese and strawbettery or raspberry jam on a toasted English muffin. Soften cream cheese with ¼ t. lemon juice by whipping with electric mixer. Serve open faced.

GREASE PAINT SANDWICHES
Cut sliced bread into an equal number of rounds and triangles. Spread with peanut butter. Place a triangle at the top of a round as a hat on top of a clown's face. Decorate the "face" with strawberry jam, raisins, cut-up maraschino cherries and red coconut.

GUESS WHAT? SANDWICHES
Place a muffin tin in the center of the table. Fill with tuna, egg salad, shredded cheese, cold cuts, peanut

butter, cream cheese, jam, jelly, deviled ham, chicken salad, etc.

Fill a basket with a variety of breads and crackers (i.e., rye, white, wheat, saltines, etc.). Let the children create their own masterpieces!

PB & ? SANDIES

PB & J (peanut butter and jelly) sandies are renowned winners with preschoolers. Here ar some variations that can be highly successful as well as nutritious.

peanut butter & cream cheese
peanut butter & grated carrots
peanut butter & applesauce
peanut butter, bacon bits & honey
peanut butter & banana slices
peanut butter & mayonnaise

PUMPKIN SAND-WITCHES

Make your favorite pumpkin bread recipe. Slice to desired thickness and spread each slice with peanut butter and orange marmalade or cream cheese whipped with lemon juice and powdered sugar to taste.

TEATIME SANDWICHES

Trim crust of an equal number of slices of whole wheat and white bread. Using cookie cutters, cut desired shapes (one white, one wheat). Spread white slice with desired filling and top with matching shape from wheat slice.

Suggested shapes: animals, hearts, flowers, shamrocks, eggs, stars, etc.

Suggested fillings: egg salad, tuna, peanut butter and jelly, chopped ham.

SLOPPY JOES

(Makes 6)

1 lb. ground beef
1 cup chopped green onions
1 cup chopped celery
small can chopped olives
1 T. brown sugar
2 T. mustard
1 cup catsup
1 T. vinegar
dash salt
hamburger buns or English muffins
  Brown hamburger. Drain. Add next 8 ingredients.
Mix. Simmer. Serve over toasted buns.

TACOS/BURRITOS

  You may wish to assemble this yourself or put the
following in bowls and have the kids "go for it!"

browned, crumbled and drained hamburger
   (1 lb. makes 8)
shredded cheddar cheese
chopped lettuce
diced tomatoes
corn or flour tortillas

  Fry corn tortillas in a hot skillet with 1″ of oil or
fat—a few seconds on each side. Remove, drain and fold.
They can be made ahead of time and kept warm in the
oven, or you may wish to use prepared "taco shells."
Another convenient variation is *burritos*, which differ
in that you use flour tortillas. Wrap the tortillas tightly in
aluminum foil and bake for 15 minutes at 400°F. until
soft and steamy. Fill with heated refried beans, or
browned hamburger and cheese, lettuce and tomatoes.
Fold or roll. Serve.

TERRIFIC TURNOVERS
Roll out a refrigerator biscuit (available in a can) with a rolling pin. Place a small (silver-dollar size) *cooked* hamburger patty in the middle with a teaspoon of Thousand Island dressing. Cover with another rolled-out biscuit and crimp the edges. Bake accoding to the directions on the biscuit can.

Variations: Try barbecue sauce, taco sauce, pizza sauce, etc., or substitute sausage, half a fish stick, tuna, cheese, etc. for the hamburger.

TUNA BURGERS/TUNA BOATS
Butter hamburger buns or hot dog buns (boats) and lightly toast. Fill with your chosen tuna mixture, sprinkle with grated cheese and bake until cheese melts in a 450°F. oven. Serve warm but not hot, as hot cheese on the roof of a child's mouth could be disastrous.

TUNA SALAD
Tuna is another winner with children as long as you don't spice it too much. We suggest mixing well-drained tuna with either mayonnaise, salad dressing or sour cream. You may wish to add a little pickle relish but watch out, kids are picky.

WITCHES' BREW
Serve your favorite soup recipe in a large bowl that has been lowered into a hollowed-out pumpkin. Sprinkle with oyster crackers or croutons. Serve in styrofoam cups.

GOOD-FOR-YA'S

ANIMAL SALAD
Place a bed of shredded lettuce on a salad plate. Put a small scoop of cottage cheese in the center. Decorate

146

with carrot or celery for ears, peach slice for smile, raisins for eyes, an olive for a nose and julienne celery for whiskers.

ANGELED EGGS

Hard boil eggs (10 minutes), drain, cover with cold water. When cool, peel and cut in half *crosswise*. Slice a bit off the bottom of each half so it will stand up. Put the yolks in a bowl and mix with mayonnaise or sour cream until smooth and thick. Fill each white with the yolk mixture and top with a pitted black olive.

ANTIPASTO

Put some of the following on each plate or arrange on a tray: olives, celery (stuffed with cheese or peanut butter), raisins, salami slices rolled and pinned with toothpick, carrot curls (wash and peel carrot, then slice as thin as possible lengthwise—curl with toothpick and put in ice water overnight—remove toothpick), hard-boiled egg slices, cucumber slices. Garnish with parsley or carrot tops.

APPLE RINGS

Core an apple, leaving a wide cavity. Fill with peanut butter or prepared cheese spread. Slice horizontally and sprinkle the apple lightly with salt or lemon juice to prevent it from turning brown. Cover and refrigerate.

BANANASHIPS

Peel a whole banana, dip in milk and roll in any of the following: granola, graham cracker crumbs, crushed nuts or flaked coconut. Place on waxed paper to dry.

Variations: Sliced bananas, banana on a stick

147

GARBAGE CAN LIDS
Thinly slice cored apples horizontally. Spread peanut butter or cheese spread on one slice and top with another slice of apple.

ROASTED PUMPKIN SEEDS
3 cups pumpkin seeds
3 T. butter
1½ t. salt
Wash the seeds thoroughly. Drain them in a colander and use paper towels to pat them dry. Sauté the above ingredients in a skillet until they are thoroughly mixed and all the seeds are coated with the butter. Spread them out on a cookie sheet and bake at 275°F. for 40 minutes, checking occasionally until they are brown.

SAFARI SALAD
Mix your favorite flavor gelatin dessert mix (keeping in mind your color scheme) in the blender, substituting yogurt for the cold water. Add drained fruit, fresh or canned. Blend until smooth and pour into a mold or into individual clear plastic cups. Refrigerate until firm. Serve.

STUFFED CELERY
Wash and remove the strings from celery and stuff them with peanut butter, cream cheese, peanut butter/cream cheese mixture, American cheese spread, tuna salad, etc.

SUNSHINE SALAD
Cut an orange in half and hollow it out. Fill with a fruit compote using fruit cocktail and adding any fresh fruits in season. The orange half serves as a dish or the salad may be placed in a wide-mouthed stemmed glass.

TEPEE TREATS
Nuts and raisins served in ice cream cone.

TRAIL MIX
1 cup shelled sunflower seeds
1 cup shelled pumpkin seeds
2 cups raisins
1 cup chopped dried fruit (apricots, pineapple,
    dates, etc.)
½ cup shredded coconut
1 cup mixed cereal (Cheerios, Wheat Chex,
    Rice Chex, etc.)
1 cup carob chips or chocolate chips

Mix together and store in air-tight container. You may omit ingredients or add others to your liking.

TROPICAL FRUIT
Buy a package of short bamboo skewers (available at most grocery stores) and spear pineapple chunks, banana slices, mandarin oranges, and any other tropical fruit in season. We don't recommend skewers for very young children. Be careful!

WHAT'S NEXT SALAD
Using paper cups, fill ¼ of each cup with strawberry gelatin. Chill until firm. Add a little vanilla yogurt and slice bananas to cover. Add another thicker layer of flavored gelatin and chill until firm. Top with more of yogurt and chopped nuts.

TRICKY TREATS

CHOCOLATE TOASTIES
This is a take-off on the old campfire favorite, S'mores.

Toast a marshmallow, dip in chocolate sauce and roll in graham cracker crumbs.

Eat right off the stick!

Sauce: Melt and stir: 1 chocolate bar
                        1 T. whole milk

Variations: Roll in granola, crispy rice cereal, sweetened wheat germ, crushed nuts, coconut

FINGER GELATIN DESSERT
1 large box gelatin dessert mix
1 small box gelatin dessert mix
1 box (4 envelopes) unflavored gelatin
4 cups boiling water

Thoroughly mix the above ingredients and pour into a large (9″ × 13″) baking pan. Chill until firm. Cut into squares or cut shapes with cookie cutters.

FUDGIES
1 pkg. chocolate pudding mix
3½ cups skim milk
1 egg

Follow directions on pudding mix box. Sweeten as desired. Freeze in ice cube trays.

GELATIN EGGS
Poke a hole at one end of a raw egg, using a small nail. The hole should be large enough so that a small funnel can fit. Shake out the egg until the shell is emptied. (Save the insides for scrambled eggs or baking.) Rinse out the eggshell with water. Fill with finger gelatin dessert recipe. Replace filled egg in the carton, hole side up. Refrigerate overnight. For serving, peel off the shell and serve.

POPCORN BALLS
1 T. butter
1 cup sugar
1½ cups light corn syrup
1 t. vanilla
½ t. salt
4 quarts popped corn
food coloring (optional)

150

Melt butter. Add sugar, corn syrup, vanilla and salt. On medium heat, boil to very hard ball stage (260°F.). Stir while pouring syrup mixture over popped corn. Butter your hands and shape mixture into balls and place on waxed paper. Makes 12 to 14 balls.

SNOW CONES
Put a large (12 oz.) can of frozen fruit juice concentrate in the blender and fill container with ice cubes. Blend until the desired consistency is reached. Serve in paper cups or paper cones.

Paper Cones: Cut a paper circle 12" in diameter. Fold in quarters. Open one thickness.

SPECIAL CUPCAKES
Bake cupcakes in greased cupcake tins. Cool. Slice off the top just under the rim. Scoop out a little cake with a spoon (pop in your mouth!) and fill cavity with pudding, jelly, fruit pie filling, applesauce, etc. Replace the top and frost as usual.

YIPES STRIPES GELATIN
A gelatin recipe this long? Could it possibly be worth it? Absolutely! This is a layered "finger" gelatin with creamy white layers in between. Choose your colors to complement your color scheme: red and blue for the All-American jamboree; red and green for Christmas; etc.

6 pkgs. unflavored gelatin
4 3-oz. boxes of flavored gelatin, each a
    different flavor and color
1 cup sweetened condensed milk
water

Lightly grease a 9" x 13" x 2" glass baking dish. Mix one package unflavored gelatin with ¼ cup tap water. In another bowl, add ¾ cup boiling water to one 3-ounce box of flavored gelatin. Mix both gelatins together. Pour

151

into the glass baking dish and refrigerate. Make sure your refrigerator rack is level. It should take about 30 minutes for each layer to become firm.

For the white layers, mix two packages of unflavored gelatin with ½ cup of tap water. Then mix in 1 cup sweetened condensed milk with 1½ cups boiling water. Stir all ingredients thoroughly. This mixture will make three layers. Cool the white mixture and pour slightly less than 1 cup on top of the chilled colored layer. Replace in refrigerator and chill until firm. Put remaining white mixture in a warm place so that it won't gel. If it begins to gel, place in a warm oven (250°F.) until it thins out.

Make your next colored layer following the same directions as above. Make sure you don't pour a very hot mixture on top of the chilled layer, as they might melt together.

Alternate the colored and white layers. You will have four colored layers and three white layers. Cut in small squares or with cookie cutters.

STUFF-ON-A-STICK

Give children something on a stick and they are in heaven. What was food now becomes a prized possession. We have gathered together some of our favorite suggestions for handle ideas. (Keep in mind the weight of the food when choosing a handle.) Use:

straws
popsicle sticks
tongue depressors
wooden ice cream spoons
licorice loops
peppermint sticks
lollipops
pipe cleaners

FREEZER POPS
1 pkg. gelatin dessert mix
1 small pkg. beverage powder
4 cups fruit juice

Dissolve gelatin in 2 cups hot juice. Mix in powder. Add 2 cups cold juice and freeze in cups. Makes 18 pops.

FROZEN BANANA
Cut a banana in half crosswise, put on a stick, wrap in waxed paper and freeze.

FRUIT-TAIL POPS
Spoon fruit cocktail into small (3½ oz.) paper or plastic cups. Add 1 t. water. Stand a small plastic spoon or wooden popsicle stick in each. Freeze. Remove from cups to serve. A standard 17-oz. can makes about eight pops.

LOLLIPOPS
Use looped pipe cleaners as sticks. Lightly butter strips of waxed paper and arrange looped pipe cleaners according to the size and number of desired lollipops.
¼ cup margarine
½ cup light corn syrup
⅞ cup sugar
food coloring

Combine all of the above ingredients except the food coloring in a large, heavy saucepan. Heat over medium to medium-high heat to boiling, occasionally stirring. Turn heat down to medium and stir continually until 270°F. is reached on a candy thermometer. Add food coloring to desired shade.

Drop this mixture onto the greased sheets of waxed paper at ends of pipe cleaners. Cool thoroughly before removing from paper.

Variation: To make "magnifying glasses," bend

153

the pipe cleaners in the shape of magnifying glasses and pour candy in the middle. Don't add food coloring.

POPCORN-POPS
Make the popcorn ball mixture (page 150). Shape it around lollipops, candy canes, peppermint sticks or wooden ice cream spoons.

ICE CREAM DESSERTS

CLOWN CONES
Cover a small (4" × 4") piece of cardboard with foil—one for each child. On top of the foil, thickly sprinkle a circle of grated coconut.* On top of the coconut, place a scoop of vanilla ice cream. Decorate the ice cream like a clown's face (use raisins, nuts, cherries, chocolate chips, etc.), and top with a sugar cone for a hat.

FLOWERPOT ICE CREAM
At your local nursery or dime store, purchase as many terra cotta or plastic flowerpots as you have children. These pots are referred to as "thumb pots." Place a

*To color coconut, place in a small bowl and add a few drops of food coloring. Mix with a spoon. Keep adding food coloring until desired shade is reached.

small piece of aluminum foil inside the pot to cover the drain hole. Fill the pot with softened ice cream. Use chocolate to resemble earth or mint to resemble grass. For each pot, make two construction paper flowers and glue the edges together except for a small portion at the bottom. Use a peppermint stick as the flower stem. Insert the peppermint stick into the open portion of the flower and "plant" the other end in the ice cream. Freeze until it is time to serve.

HOMEMADE ICE CREAM BARS
Scoop ice cream balls into cupcake papers. Turn onto an aluminum foil-lined cookie sheet and stick a wooden popsicle stick through bottom of cup. Refreeze.

A treat would be to sprinkle the ice cream with nuts, candy, etc. before turning over.

ICE CREAM OR YOGURT BALLS
Scoop out ice cream balls and place in foil or paper cupcake cups. Place on a cookie sheet, cover with plastic wrap and freeze. This way you won't have to scoop while children are anxiously awaiting dessert.

Before freezing, you may wish to decorate with candy sprinkles, nuts, raisins, M & M's, etc.

ICE CREAM SANDIES
Be innovative and try making your own ice cream sandwiches! You can use any flavor ice cream, frozen yogurt or sherbet as the filling. For the sandwich, try ginger snaps, vanilla wafers, oatmeal or chocolate chip cookies, chocolate or plain graham crackers, or waffles. Wrap individually in aluminum foil and freeze. To make the sandwiches especially festive, tie a ribbon or yarn around each wrapped sandwich and serve like a present.

INDIVIDUAL ICE CREAM PIES

Press 2 T. graham cracker mixture—1¼ cups (16 graham crackers) crumbs, 1 T. sugar, ¼ cup melted butter or margarine—into paper-lined muffin tin cups. Fill with softened ice cream, yogurt or sherbet (any flavor). Sprinkle with nuts, chocolate syrup, strawberry topping, jam, fresh fruit or any other variation you may come up with. Refreeze.

Variation: Use prepared individual-size graham cracker crumb tart shells, and proceed as above.

MAKE-A-SUNDAE

Children really enjoy experimenting and creating, especially if you make it extra special by providing them with plastic banana split boats purchased either in the paper products section of your grocery store or from a local ice cream franchise. Or you can buy inexpensive plastic toy sailboats from a variety store. Remove the sail, make the sundae and replace sail. After the children have consumed their ice cream concoction, wash out the sailboat and send it home as a party favor.

Concoction suggestions: (Use vanilla ice cream or yogurt.) Fresh fruits, bananas, applesauce, jams, prepared ice cream toppings, chocolate, carob or butterscotch chips, M & M's, nuts, marshmallows, raisins, granola, graham cracker crumbs, and more!!

PERFECT PARFAITS

Layer either frozen yogurt or ice cream with fresh fruit: bananas, strawberries, cinnamoned apples (use any one fruit or a combination). Consider color as well as taste.

RAGGEDY ANN CONES

Place a scoop of vanilla ice cream in a standard flat-bottomed ice cream cone. Decorate with cinnamon hearts for eyes and mouth and red coconut for hair. You can get as fancy and creative as you choose. Cover lightly with plastic wrap and keep in freezer until serving time.

(*Hint:* Put them in a muffin tin to keep them upright!)

SNOWBALLS
Roll a scoop of ice cream around in a bowl filled with coconut and place in a cupcake paper. Place scoops on cookie sheet, cover with waxed paper and freeze. (Decorate with holly leaves and a candy cane at Christmas time.)

TODDLER ICE CREAM
Mix:
½ can sweetened condensed milk
1½ T. cocoa
½ cup milk

Place mixture in freezer for 2 hours. Remove and whip. Pour into ice cube tray. Place cube divider in tray. Freeze for 2-3 more hours.

YOGURT POPS
1 carton plain yogurt (8 oz.)
1 6-oz. can concentrated fruit juice
dash vanilla or honey

Mix and freeze in an ice cube tray or in 3-oz. paper cups.

A simpler version is to just use flavored yogurt and omit juice.

CAKES AND COOKIES

Even when the party is not a birthday celebration, children won't feel it is complete without a cake. With each of our theme parties we have tried to give an alternative dessert idea, plus a traditional cake. Most children enjoy the frosting and decoration more than the cake itself, so we suggest you conserve your energy and use a cake mix. A handy trick to make a cake mix moister is to substitute ¼ cup oil for ¼ cup of the called-for-water. It will taste homemade, we promise! If you have the time and inclination, however, we offer a few nutritious cake recipes, along with some for cookies.

The variously shaped cakes are best served on a large piece of cardboard* covered with brightly colored wrapping paper, wallpaper or foil. Or you can cover a cookie sheet with wrapping paper (just tape it on the bottom).

Before frosting a cake, place pieces of waxed paper just under the edge to protect your serving platter. When you finish frosting, slide the waxed paper out and throw it away.

Several of our special cakes call for one-layer, round cakes. Most children, especially younger ones, will be too excited at a party to eat much cake. We suggest you make a one-layer cake mix. For larger parties, make a two-layer mix and pour the second half into cupcake tins.

Every birthday cake needs candles. Try securing the candles with Lifesavers, gumdrops or miniature marshmallows. These can also be used to spell out your child's name on the cake, or you may wish to do this in frosting. The prepared frosting in decorating tubes (available at the supermarket) works well, or you can make a frosting tube with waxed paper.

Tear off a 12″-piece of waxed paper. Fold in half, and then in half again. Then fold diagonally. Snip off a

---

*Cut a piece from a large box, use the lid to a large box, call a pizza parlor and offer to buy a round (and hope they offer you one for free!) or try a craft store that carries cake decorating equipment.

tiny piece of the folded corner. Fill with frosting and squeeze.

AMERICAN FLAG CAKE

Bake your cake in a 9″ × 13″ cake pan. Prepare butter cream frosting. Divide the frosting in three small bowls. Color one bowl blue and one red. Use lots of food coloring; the darker the better. Spread blue frosting in the upper left hand corner of the cake. Put the white frosting in a pastry tube with a star tip. Make white stars on the blue square. Put a wide slit tip on the pastry tube with more white frosting and make the white stripes. Make the red stripes in the same fashion. Finish off the cake by putting "sparklers" or birthday candles in some of the stars.

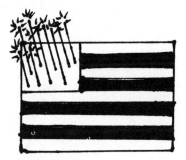

ANIMAL CRACKERS

Use either store-bought animal cookies or use the Sugar Cookie recipe on page 168 cut into animal shapes. Drizzle with icing.

APPLESAUCE CAKE

2½ cups flour
1 cup sugar
1 cup brown sugar
1½ t. baking powder
1½ t. salt

¾ t. cinnamon
½ t. allspice
1½ cups canned applesauce
½ cup water
½ cup shortening
2 eggs
1 cup raisins

Blend all ingredients (except raisins) with mixer for 3 minutes. Fold in raisins with a spoon. Pour into greased and floured pans. Bake at 350°F. for 60 minutes in oblong (9″ × 13″) pans or 50 minutes in two 8″ layer pans. Cool and frost (see Carrot Cake frosting).

BOXCAR CAKE
Bake a 9″ × 13″ rectangular cake. Cool and remove from pan. Frost with dark chocolate frosting. Add the "boxcar" effect with white tube frosting. Use commercial chocolate cupcakes for the wheels.

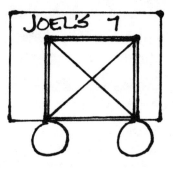

CAROUSEL CAKE
Bake a two–layer round cake. Cool and frost. Decorate the sides with frosted animal cookies (packaged or homemade). Stand eight 4″ peppermint sticks in a circle on top of the cake and top with a paper dome:
Cut an 11″-diameter circle from an 11″ x 15″ piece of construction paper. Cut a slit halfway through, overlap 2″ and tape.

160

CARROT CAKE
 Sift together in bowl:
2 cups flour
2 t. baking powder
1½ t. baking soda
2 t. cinnamon
1 t. salt
2 cups sugar

 Add:
1½ cups oil
4 eggs (beaten slightly)
3 cups grated carrots
½ cup chopped nuts

Mix and pour into greased 9″ × 13″ pan.

 Bake at 350°F. for 45 minutes. Try making carrot cupcakes . . . The kids will love them plain or frosted.

FROSTING:
1 cup powdered sugar
4 oz. cream cheese
4 T. butter
1 t. vanilla
¼ cup coconut
¼ cup chopped nuts

 Cream sugar, cheese and butter until smooth. Add vanilla, and stir in. Add coconut and nuts.

CARROT COOKIES

1 cup shortening (or ½ cup margarine
   plus ½ cup shortening)
2 cups flour
⅓ cup sugar (or ¼ cup white sugar
   plus ¼ cup brown sugar)
½ t. salt
½ t. cinnamon
1 t. vanilla
1 egg
1 cup grated raw carrots

Cream shortening. Sift flour, sugar, salt and cinnamon together. Add to shortening and mix. Add vanilla, egg and carrots and mix again. Turn on lightly floured board. Roll into a long tube. Wrap in waxed paper and chill. When ready to bake, slice and place on ungreased cookie sheet. Bake at 375°F. for 10 minutes.

CLOWN CAKE

Pour your favorite cake mix into one square pan and one round pan, making sure that batter height is equal. Reserve enough batter and fill one cupcake cup.* Bake as directed on package. After cooling, cut cake as shown in drawing. Arrange cake pieces on a 22″ × 26″ piece of cardboard covered with brightly colored paper. Frost the cake pieces with white frosting, decorate face with large and small multicolored gumdrops. Dot bow tie with small gumdrops. Use colored (yellow or red) shredded coconut around cap for hair. Decorate pompon (cupcake) with colored gumdrops.

*Foil cupcake cups can be placed in oven without a muffin tin.

162

CLUE COOKIES
½ cup soft margarine
¾ cup sifted powdered sugar
1 T. vanilla
1½ cups sifted flour
⅛ t. salt

Heat oven to 350°F. Mix margarine, sugar and vanilla. Then blend in flour and salt with hands. Wrap a tablespoon of dough around your "surprise" and bake 1″ apart on ungreased cookie sheet for 12 to 15 minutes.

Surprise suggestions: Chocolate kisses, a nut, a mint, cherry, date, M & M, gumdrop, etc.

CUPCAKE BASKETS
Make your favorite cupcake recipe. Frost with either chocolate or white frosting. Sprinkle heavily with green colored coconut. The shredded coconut mixed with a few drops of green food coloring will resemble grass. Place three jelly beans in the "grass." Bend a pipe

163

cleaner and place each end in the cupcake to look like a handle.

DETECTIVE'S ID CAKE

Using your child's favorite flavor cake mix, make a sheet cake following recipe instructions on the package. After removing cooled cake from pan, frost with white frosting. Using prepared tube frosting of your chosen colors, make a border around the edges of the cake, place candles at top and decorate as shown in drawing.

DOLL CARRIAGE CAKE

Bake a one-layer round white cake plus two cupcakes. Add food coloring to tint the cake to carry out your color scheme. After the round layer has thoroughly cooled, cut away ¼ as shown in the diagram. Assemble the carriage with cupcake wheels. Frost and decorate.

164

GINGERBREAD CAKE
1 cup brown sugar
1 cup butter or shortening
3 eggs (well beaten)
1 cup molasses
1 t. soda (dissolved in 1 t. warm water)
1 t. ginger
1 t. cinnamon
3 cups flour (sifted)
1 cup sour cream

Cream sugar and butter. Add eggs, molasses, soda and spices. Add flour alternately with sour cream. Blend. Bake 30 minutes at 350°F. in greased 9" × 13" pan.

HEART CAKE
Bake a two-layer cake. Make one layer in a round pan, the other in a square pan. Pour batter so that both are the same height.

Cover an 18"-square piece of cardboard with red-and-white wrapping paper and a white doily. When cake is thoroughly cooled, cut and shape as in the diagram, and frost.

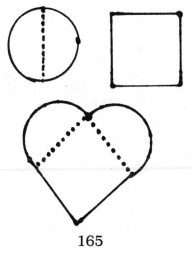

JACK-O-LANTERN CAKE

Bake a one-layer yellow cake in a round pan. Add a little extra yellow food coloring to the mix. Cool the cake thoroughly. Use a sharp, pointed knife to "carve" two eyes and a mouth. Save the eyes to form the stem, as shown in the diagram. Brush away the crumbs before frosting the pumpkin orange and the stem green.

NUT TORTE
2 T. flour
2½ t. baking powder
4 eggs
¾ cup sugar
1 cup nuts, chopped fine

Pour mixture into two 8"-square greased cake pans. Bake 20 minutes at 350°F. Frost between layers and on the top only with whipped cream. Sprinkle with chocolate sprinkles.

OLYMPIAD CAKE

Bake your choice of cake in a rectangular pan. Cool and frost. Decorate with the Olympic insignia.

166

PETITS FOURS

Prepare a pound cake batter. Pour into greased and floured jelly roll pan, 15½″ × 10½″ × 1″. Bake approximately 25 minutes. Cool. Cut cake into fancy shapes using cookie cutters.

Petits Fours Icing:
9 cups sifted confectioner's sugar
½ cup water
½ cup light corn syrup
¾ t. vanilla
½ t. almond extract

Combine and heat icing ingredients in top of double boiler until icing is lukewarm. Remove from heat, keeping icing over hot water.

Using a fork to hold cake piece, spoon the icing over each. Using another fork, push glazed piece off onto wire rack to set glaze.

Icing may be tinted in pastel colors.

Decorate with peppermint drops, silver sprinkles, etc.

ROCKET CAKE

Bake your child's favorite flavor cake in two square pans. Cool sufficiently and cut according to diagram. Arrange on cardboard covered with foil. Frost with yellow or white icing and decorate with silver colored candies and your child's name.

167

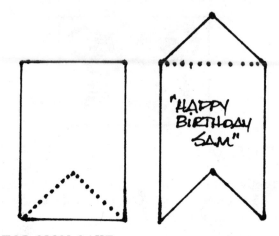

STOP SIGN CAKE
Bake two square layers. Trim the corners to resemble a stop sign. Frost with red and white frosting.

SUGAR COOKIES
¾ cup margarine
2 eggs
1¼ cups sugar
1 t. vanilla
2¼ cups all-purpose flour
1 t. baking powder
¾ t. salt

Mix margarine, eggs, sugar and vanilla. Blend in other ingredients and chill for one hour.

Roll out dough, cut and place on ungreased cookie sheet. Bake at 400°F. for 5 to 7 minutes.

TIN CAN CUPCAKES
Using your favorite cupcake or cake recipe, fill a clean, greased and floured 10½-oz. tuna can ¼ full. Bake at 350°F. for 15 minutes. Top with ice cream and chocolate sprinkles (to resemble dirt). Serve.

TOTEM POLE CAKE
Bake one 9″ × 13″ layer cake. Cut according to diagram after cake is thoroughly cooled. Frost each section with a different color and decorate with Indian symbols.

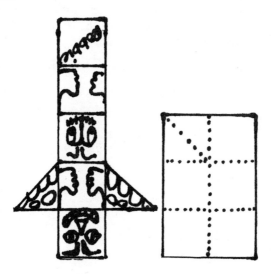

We hope we have given you some ideas, inspiration and courage. At this point, our husbands felt we should offer the standard, "Take two aspirin and go to bed"! We lean toward our earlier advice to get a babysitter and go out for a quiet dinner. You deserve it.

The Authors

Index